CONFESSIONS OF A NOMAD

CONFESSIONS OF A NOMAD

A Devotional Guide

By William L. Self
And Carolyn Shealy Self

PEACHTREE PUBLISHERS, LTD.

Published by
PEACHTREE PUBLISHERS, LTD.
494 Armour Circle, N. E.
Atlanta, Georgia 30324

Manufactured in the United States of America

Text and Cover Design by Cindy McDaniel

ISBN: 0-931948-47-9
Library of Congress Catalog Card Number 83-61913

DEDICATION

Dedicated to the congregation of the Wieuca Road Baptist Church, Atlanta, Georgia — our fellow travelers through the deserts and oases of life.

IN APPRECIATION

We want to express our deep appreciation for the typing and proofreading of these dear friends: Norma and Bill Key, Christi Key, Miriam Childs, Betsy Hollis, Pat Rice, and Bryan Self. We also appreciate the help with naming the book from Pam Nolen.

A WORD FROM THE AUTHORS

Our fascination with Moses, the Sinai, and the book of Exodus began in 1978, when we were first introduced to the compelling forces of this unusual desert. Twice we have made the trip from Elat, along the Gulf of Aqaba and deep into the Sinai Peninsula, to Mount Sinai and the fourteen-hundred-year-old Monastery of St. Catherine.

As we turned off the well-traveled coastal highway during our last trip, dust filled our bus and forced us to tie scarves and handkerchiefs around our heads for protection. We looked like bandits as we followed the primitive road signs — only piles of rocks stacked along the side of the road — for direction. Our road was a *wadi*, a dried up river bed, which, we had been told, could flood with only a little rain, forcing us to scale the rocky cliffs around us to escape. In the distance, we could see an oasis with Bedouin tents and camels silhouetted on the horizon.

Some of our group were ill at ease and fretful because of the overwhelming sense of the unknown. It seemed to us, however, that we had been there before. We felt an indescribable sense of God's presence in the vast sands of this desert, the jagged peaks, and barren ridges; in the beauty of the colored sands, which had been swept into unique formations by the wind; and in the snowy whiteness of the cumulus clouds in the azure sky. We could almost see that ragtag brood, whom Moses led out of Egypt, as they camped along the way. We felt that we could hear them as they sat around the campfire, grumbling and worrying about tomorrow.

The bleakness, the beauty, the vastness, and even the mystery were somehow familiar to us. You see, we've traveled the deserts of life; we've been on the backside of God's mountain. It was familiar territory to us, because we had walked other raw landscapes in our lives.

As God had used the desert experience to mature a nation, God uses life's deserts to mature His dear ones. We had gratefully accepted, for our own lives, the promise that God gave to Moses, as recorded in Exodus 33:14: "My Presence will go with you, and I will give you rest." Somehow, there is comfort in knowing that even the great Moses was lonely and sometimes frightened. But God took care of the loneliness of Moses with His presence, and He showed His understanding of human nature by saying, "I will give you rest." This rest is not a stagnation, but the kind of rest that comes when we've been challenged and stretched; and because of this mental and spiritual growth, we're able to appreciate and receive more of the treasures that God has ready for us.

Moses grew from a shepherd on the backside of God's mountain to become the medium through whom the covenant between God and the Israelites was concluded. God uses people today, just as surely as He worked wonders through Moses. Place yourself in the dialogue that was spoken between these two, and the reward can be yours: "The Lord would speak to Moses face to face, as a man speaks with his friend."

William L. Self
Carolyn Shealy Self

October, 1983

CONTENTS

FRESH EVERY MORNING

A TREASURED POSSESSION

REQUIREMENTS FOR COMMITMENT

THE DARKNESS WHERE GOD WAS

THE PATHWAY UPWARD

VOICES OF OUR DAY

THE SEARCH FOR WHOLENESS

Scripture references taken from New International Version, Zondervan Bible Publishers, Grand Rapids, Michigan.

ALL-POWERFUL GOD

1. He Is in Control

Genesis 1:1-2 *In the beginning, God created the heavens and the earth. Now the earth was formless and empty, darkness was over the surface of the deep, and the Spirit of God was hovering over the waters.*

There is a feeling in the world today that God is not all-powerful. Somehow, we feel that God stands and bows before all the great technological advances of mankind. Man's amazing conquests in space and the development of wonder drugs and treatments — for diseases such as tuberculosis, smallpox, and cancer — make us feel that God must somehow bring Himself into alignment with our brilliance. Perhaps it is asking a lot for us to acknowledge that God is all-powerful, in light of modern accomplishments.

The message in the opening verses of the Bible clearly states that God was in control then. The rest of His word assures us that He controls history, nature, and mankind. God is unquestionably sovereign. The Spirit of God is always hovering over our lives. Will you be aware of Him and let Him be free to create a new joy in your life?

Prayer: *O Father, creator of all the universe, be all-powerful in my life. Let me acknowledge again my trust in You. You, who made the delicate hummingbirds and butterflies, also made me. You care for the birds and butterflies, and I can trust You with my life. The creator does not destroy, but allows me to find ways to serve. Create in me a clean heart, a joyous heart, O Father. Amen.*

ALL-POWERFUL GOD

2. Slavery Is No Fun

Exodus 1:8-14 *Then a new king, who did not know about Joseph, came to power in Egypt. (v.8) . . . in all their hard labor, the Egyptians used them ruthlessly. (v.14b)*

The Hebrews had come to Egypt to escape the famine. Joseph was already there, having risen from slavery to a powerful government position. The Hebrews prospered for several generations, then a new king who didn't know about Joseph came into power. He felt the Hebrews were a threat to him and decided to make them slaves. One day they were free, then the next day they were ruthlessly oppressed.

Are you in bondage? Are you a slave? Many of us live as did those enslaved Hebrews. Some are wincing under the lashes of such slave masters as a bad marriage, unreconciled grief, economic disaster, and illness. Be assured that there is deliverance. The mighty God who brought you to the face of this earth, the mighty God who loves you and cares for you, the mighty God who is the author of deliverance is with you now. God provides a way out.

Remember that the Hebrew people did not die in bondage. They grew strong and prospered, even in persecution. So can you. You *can* develop new strength and new hope and be delivered from your Egypt.

Prayer: *O God, give me strength and courage to be delivered from bondage. I am miserable, bleeding from the lashes of the Egyptians in my life. Begin now to heal the wounds, and lead me out of this desperate situation. Thank You for loving and caring for me, regardless of my condition. Amen.*

ALL-POWERFUL GOD

3. Why Me, O Lord?

Exodus 2:23-25 *God heard their groaning and He remembered . . . and was concerned about them. (vv.24a, 25b)*

When the word groaning is used in the Bible, you can be sure that it's more than just a sigh or an "oh, me." It's a sound that comes from the very depths of the soul. It is a desperate cry.

Imagine the Hebrew people. Can't you see a successful shopkeeper suddenly taken into slavery and sent down to the city of Ramses to build the granaries? Can't you feel the groaning of his soul at night, when he sees his wife and children as slaves? At night they all return from the work camps with barely enough strength to start the fire and cook a meager meal. Can't you hear their groanings? Can't you hear their questions? Why did this happen to my family and my people? What did I do to deserve this? How can God allow this to happen to *me*?

Are you also groaning? Your marriage of twenty years is over. You got off to a good start, because you loved each other completely, but you couldn't look down the road to see the changes that would destroy the marriage.

Are you groaning? You had a good job and a bright future with a successful company. Nobody told you that, when you reached middle age, the company would be sold to a "new king who didn't know Joseph." Now your career is on the shelf, and you're caught in a kind of economic bondage.

God hears your groanings; He sees your misery. Now you must ask for His help and strength. Remember that you are not the only person in an Egypt. You are in the company of many good people whose lives have crumbled. "So God looked on the Israelites and was concerned about them."

Prayer: *Put your name in place of "the Israelites," and know that God cares for you. Remember to thank Him for caring.*

3

ALL-POWERFUL GOD

4. Nobody Knows the Trouble I've Seen

Exodus 3:7 *The Lord said, "I have indeed seen the misery of my people in Egypt. I have heard them crying out because of their slave drivers, and I am concerned about their suffering."*

Misery is a condition that often comes when our convenant with God is broken. As we become slaves to such weaknesses as anger, a bad disposition, an unnecessarily harsh tongue, or lustful desires that get out of hand, we make ourselves miserable. We all can make a list of the ways we have become enslaved.

The covenant is an interesting thing, and something we should not take casually. It is the contract between God and his people, and God never severs that contract. God is always faithful. He says many times in Genesis and throughout the Old Testament, "Be faithful to me and I'll be your God." He did not break the contract. When the Hebrew people began to remember the covenant and called on Him, God heard their cries of anguish and saw their misery. He addressed himself to their plight.

Many people get upset because they have broken the covenant. They had been washed in the blood of Jesus Christ (the New Covenant), but now they fear that they've been thrown out of the family. Remember that the covenant is still in operation. You don't lose it simply because it has been dulled in your mind. God wants to deliver you from bondage, as He did the Hebrews. It seems that we have to be very miserable before we allow Him to deliver us.

Prayer: *"Out of my bondage, sorrow and strife . . ."* Dear Father, we *want deliverance; we need deliverance. You know the areas of bondage in my life. Please direct me to the people who can help me. Deliver me from bad influences and give me courage and determination to depend on your guidance in my life. Amen.*

ALL-POWERFUL GOD

5. Free at Last!

Exodus 3:8a *"So I have come down to rescue them from the hand of the Egyptians, and to bring them up out of that land into a good and spacious land, a land flowing with milk and honey . . ."*

The nature of God is made clear here. He is not a God of wrath; He is a God of love. The nature of God is not judgmental. He is a God who, as a loving father, cares for His people and is always aware of their circumstances. God looks with love and pity upon the people, and moves in to do what He can. He delivers from bondage in many ways, but not always by personal encounter.

Many times we have to look back over our shoulder to see how God moved to deliver us. It is not always obvious at the time. We don't know how you will be delivered from your bondage, but you can be sure that He has started the process. Jesus on the cross took His blood and shed it abroad so that you could be free. His sacrifice on the cross brings you out of your bondage. As Moses said to Pharaoh, "Let my people go," so God in Jesus says to you and to me, "Come out of the tomb, shed the grave clothes. Be whole and clean, changed and free."

Prayer: *Dear Father, thank You for providing a way out. I've been through pestilence and wilderness, and I'm so tired of wandering, always in the bonds of self-doubt and fear. Thank You for Your love and care. Thank You for hearing my cries and seeing my distress. Give me courage to accept Your way out. Amen.*

MIRACLES

6. Strength of Weakness

Exodus 1:15-21 *The midwives, however, feared God and did not do what the king of Egypt had told them to do; they let the boys live. (v.17)*

We see in this passage a highly significant theme that runs through the Old Testament. Quite simply, it's the strength of weakness and the weakness of strength. What a world we live in, where people become so confused that they think strength is everything. The biblical theme is that power is with God, and the power of the world is weak before God. We see Goliath falling before David, Daniel in the lion's den, Herod fooled by the Wise Men, Pharaoh defeated by his slaves in Egypt, and Jesus' resurrection destroying the worst power that the devil could throw against him — the power of death. All the way through the Bible, man's power and the marshalling of man's power are weak.

If you have anchored your life with the power of this world, you will be lost. Banking on money, looking for executive power, or trying to marshall the defenses of this world against evil will fail. God's power is triumphant over all powers of the world. The Bible says this again and again. God's power grows and looks weak, but it makes all the tyrants of the world tumble. Herod is in his grave, Pharaoh is mummified, but the people of God were brought out of bondage by a baby born in captivity and rescued in an ark. That baby is triumphant over all of them. Every person must come to the place where he recognizes, because of the testimony of God within, that the power of this world will not survive. The power of God survives for all eternity. We may think we don't need the power of the gospel for our lives. After all, we're self-sufficient; we can make our own decisions. We can go against whatever comes. We're well-educated, well-placed, have a good bank account, and a good marriage. But the Bible says this, too, shall pass.

Prayer: *Father, give me strength today to be a part of the true power. Let me anchor my life in Your ways. Help me to see through the sham of the world's demands so that I can love and do Your will. Amen.*

MIRACLES

7. Weakness of Strength

Exodus 2:1-10 *When the child grew older, she took him to Pharaoh's daughter, and he became her son. She named him Moses, saying, "I drew him out of the water." (v.10)*

We have seen the strength of weakness; now we're also going to see the weakness of strength. Herod and Pharaoh were strong, but even they could not stand against the innocent power of a baby born in their land. You may feel strong, and you may try to cope with difficulties in your job or your marriage. You face the Pharaohs all the time, and you try to go against them with your own power. But they still have you in slavery. Understand, however, that you do not have to face them alone. God says that He is there with you. He will bring power to bear upon the problem.

You cry out, "How is this to be? How can I go against all of these things with only an invisible strength? Hasn't God been rolled out of our society by computers? Isn't God so weak that nobody pays any attention to Him? God doesn't know how bad off I am. Why doesn't God do something about my situation?"

We suggest that you remember the mystery of the presence of God. Beware of anybody who knows everything about God. There are people who have God in a neat, little package. They know all there is to know about Him. They try to tell you why He does everything. But this scripture tells us that God works in a very mysterious way in human lives. No one — not the slaves or Pharaoh — would have said that God would work this way, until it was over and they looked back. But in the moment the slaves were crying the most, at the time their pain was at its highest level, at the time they thought God had completely turned His back upon them, what happened? God was doing something they didn't know about. It took Moses a long time to grow into manhood, go into the desert, and come back, but God was working for their salvation all of that time. God doesn't work on our timetable. God is never on schedule, but He's always on time. We can guarantee you that today God is at work in your situation, bringing it to the right conclusion, that He already has started the answer.

Prayer: *Dear Father, do something with my life. Let my weakness become Your strength. Bring power into my life so that I can serve You better through all the circumstances that I may walk. Amen.*

MIRACLES

8. Determination

Exodus 2:1-10 *But when she could hide him no longer, she got a papyrus basket for him and coated it with tar and pitch. Then she placed the child in it and put it among the reeds along the bank of the Nile. (v.3)*

The birth of Moses is a unique happening. We see a mother who would not give in to the Egyptian command that all babies were to be killed.

In order to restrict the birth of the Hebrew children, the midwives had been ordered to kill all babies at birth. They, of course, found a way not to destroy life, so Pharaoh ordered the soldiers to go into the Hebrew camp and to kill all newborn babies. Every night they went through the camp, leaving a trail of grieving families.

But there was one mother, Jochebed, who would not let this happen. Can you see her hiding her baby as the soldiers came each night? Day after day, she found ways to conceal the baby. No one could know that this baby had not been killed by soldiers.

Keeping the secret was difficult. Not only were the Egyptian soldiers who came through a problem, but there were also jealous mothers whose babies had already been killed. Finally the family realized they could not hide the baby any longer. Jochebed decided to build a boat in which to hide him. She began weaving that little ark, making it strong enough to withstand the water that would beat against it in the Nile River. Then early in the morning, she slipped her baby into the ark and placed the small vessel in the edge of the river. She instructed her daughter to watch over the baby.

What Jochebed did is an example of determination in the face of devastating circumstances. She was strong. You, too, are strong, because God made you. He didn't make you to give in to peer pressure and to go along with the gang in order to be popular. He didn't make you to give up the minute life gets tough, and things don't go your way. He made you tough enough to build an ark for survival when necessary.

Prayer: *Dear Father, give me the courage and strength of Jochebed and others who have given us the pattern of determination in the face of supreme obstacles. Help me today not to bend to pressures that would make You ashamed of me. Amen.*

8

MIRACLES

9. God Working Through People

Exodus 1:15-2:10 *Then Pharaoh's daughter went down to the Nile to bathe. . . . She opened it and saw the baby. He was crying, and she felt sorry for him. . . . Then his sister asked Pharaoh's daughter, "Shall I go and get one of the Hebrew women to nurse the baby for you?" (2:vv.5a,6a,7)*

No one achieves importance or becomes the person God wants them to be without other people. The story of Moses tells us that miracles are possible only with the help of God working through people. The fact that he lived at all was a miracle. The Hebrew midwives, who defied the Pharaoh's order to kill the babies, his mother, Jochebed, his sister Miriam, and Pharaoh's daughter all played a part in saving his life.

Miriam was a very perceptive little girl. Have you ever wondered why she was really there? Was she there to change the diaper and feed the baby, or was she there to trace the floating of the ark in the Nile? One reason she was there was to protect him from the enormous crocodiles up and down the Nile.

One morning, Pharaoh's daughter, probably the daughter of Ramses II, came down to the Nile to take a bath. Historians tell us that she was childless, so she probably was performing an act of worship to the Egyptian god of fertility. While she was there, she heard the cries of a baby. You know how the story goes. She found the baby and drew him out of the water. Miriam came and offered to find a nurse. Now, it took an intelligent child to do that. She could have run from Pharaoh's daughter, but instead she brought her mother to nurse the baby.

Moses never would have made it without the women in his life — the midwives, his mother, his sister, and Pharaoh's daughter. God used them all to give us Moses.

We are all the products of the people in our lives. We couldn't survive without special people to give us courage, hope, and love. So you *are* a miracle and also a part of someone else's miracle.

Prayer: *Thank You, heavenly Father, for the people who help me survive. (Name them.) Use me as an instrument of Your miracles. Amen.*

MIRACLES

10. The Mystery of Two Babes

Exodus 2:10; Matthew 2:1-18 *And so was fulfilled what the Lord had said through the prophet: "Out of Egypt I called my son." (Matt. 2:15b)*

God works in strange ways. He didn't begin the redemption of the world by blowing trumpets or heralding it through the palaces of kings and princes. He began in a humble stable. When God moved to bring His people out of bondage, He began in the Jewish community of Egypt with the birth of a babe.

When Moses was born, the Egyptians were talking about the conquests of the army, the wheat harvest, and the big events of the palace. They didn't notice the birth of Moses. God works in very inconspicuous ways. But that little ark that held Moses was the most important ship in all of history. It was more important than the Mayflower or the Spanish Armada, because it carried the redemption of God's people as they came out of bondage.

God's plan always hangs on a very thin thread. Would you have believed that a midwife, a little girl, and a mother with a little reed ark could save a nation? Would you have believed that a young virgin with a child in her womb could travel from Nazareth to Bethlehem to give birth to the Savior of the world? What a thin thread salvation always comes on — but not too thin to challenge the worst of tyrants. None could be more tyrannical than Pharaoh or Herod, known for killing people and driving cities into destruction, because he feared losing his throne.

Can you imagine the child Moses or the child Jesus threatening with power? You would think that a man like Pharaoh, who snapped his finger and marched armies, or a man like Herod, who had appointment from Caesar to be the ruler over all the Jews, would rest in their power. But power doesn't rest. Moses was born to deliver his people, and Jesus came to fulfill the promises of Isaiah.

There is mystery about God. He works in unusual ways. However, His care and love for each person is not a mystery. He is ready to give you the power to live today in freedom from the bondage of selfishness, hatred, and fear.

Prayer: *Dear Father, give me the strength today to take the thin thread of salvation and weave it into a strong cord of love and care for others. Amen.*

10

BURNOUT

11. Any Old Bush Will Do

Exodus 3:1-7 *There the angel of the Lord appeared to him* [Moses] *in flames of fire from within a bush. Moses saw that though the bush was on fire, it did not burn up. (v.2)*

A bush on fire that did not burn up! Now, that would be an interesting thing to see. We were with a group of people who climbed Mount Sinai several years ago. When several of us came down ahead of the main group, we huddled together for warmth as the sun went down. The desert cold began to chill our bones. We gathered some sagebrush to build a fire and soon had a pile about four feet high. We thought we had enough fuel to stay warm forever, but the fire burned bright and high for only about five minutes, and then it was absolutely gone — burned out.

That's the way life is for most people. They think they're just about to get what they need out of life, and then it disintegrates.

There is no need to debate what kind of bush burned but was not consumed. You don't need to know whether or not it was something that Moses imagined. What you need to see in this part of Scripture is that when God gets ready to do something, when God wants to reveal Himself, when God comes to give you your command, any old bush will do. You don't need a special bush. God can use the things of this world.

Look at that line — "It burned without being consumed." That's what we think we should do. Look at the tired businessman, shuffling on and off airplanes. Look at the tired mother, running through town with a station wagon full of children. Living is a depleting experience. Just getting a check cashed, or picking up your laundry, or straightening out the bills can destroy your life. It's a wonder that we get anything done in this world, but man thinks he's not consumed.

The illustration shows that God is the one who speaks through natural resources. God is the one who never has all of His being consumed. God has limitless resources, but how are we going to get by? We are the ones who are limited. The limited man comes to the limitless God, and something begins to happen.

Prayer: *Father, I am being consumed. I feel used up. Help me with these situations. Renew my strength with Your limitless resources. Amen.*

BURNOUT

12. The Backside of God's Mountain

Exodus 3:1-7 *Now Moses was tending the flock of Jethro, his father-in-law, the priest of Midian, and he led the flock to the far side of the desert and came to Horeb, the mountain of God. (v.1)*

The story of Moses is familiar to most of us. He was tending his father-in-law's sheep on the backside of the mountain of God, and he saw a bush burning but not being consumed. He heard the Lord speak to him out of that bush, telling him to take off his shoes, because he was standing on holy ground. Then God commissioned Moses for a mighty act.

Notice where Moses was. He was on the backside of God's mountain. We've been to the backside of that mountain in two ways. We have literally put our feet on that place in the Sinai, and it is desolate. We also have been there in a figurative sense. Life can be a journey over hilly terrain; it can be a journey from desert to oasis.

Some of today's theology says you're supposed to breeze through life without having any problems, if you're a Christian. But this thinking doesn't agree with the Biblical revelation. The New Testament revelation has a cross in the middle of it, followed by a resurrection. It does not depict life as always sweet and kind. It has death and depression; it has deserts and desolation; it has poverty and famine; but in the midst of all that, it has the hand of God holding everything together.

A wise king asked one of his philosophers to write the history of the world. The philosopher came in with five hundred volumes, and the king said to him, "That's not adequate. Go back and condense all that you've written into one page." The philosopher came back with this line: "This is the life experience of all men who have ever had sorrow and died." That's the history of the world. You didn't come to this point in your life without some pressure. The expression, "Everybody has his own bag of rocks around his neck," is true.

I don't know what your bag of rocks is, but everybody has one. John Bunyan had his. He was in Bedford jail for twelve years, but while he was there, God spoke to him. In the midst of that experience, he wrote *Pilgrim's Progress*. As Abraham Lincoln walked the halls of the White House, grieving over the death of his son, he found

12

Bunyan's *Pilgrim's Progress*. As he read it, he began to understand what was going on in his life.

God speaks clearest on the far side of the desert. If you need the sunlight all of the time, you do not understand the ways of God in your life.

Prayer: *Tell God how it feels to be on the backside of his mountain. Tell Him about the fears, the terrors of the night, the loneliness, the sadness, and despair. Now, be silent and let God speak to you. Hear Him say to you, as He said to Moses, "I have all that you need; I made you; I give you what you need." You need to hear that today. Amen.*

BURNOUT

13. Time to Turn Aside

Exodus 3:1-7 *So Moses thought, "I will go over and see this strange sight – why the bush does not burn up." (v.3)*

It's a good thing that Moses wasn't like modern man. He probably wouldn't have taken the time to step off the path and investigate the burning bush. God would have needed to put up a roadblock, because a modern Moses would have been too busy.

We don't step off the path much today, because we're always bent on going somewhere. Are you rushing down a dead-end street? What kind of goal are you pursuing? If you saw a burning bush, would you refuse to stop because it wasn't on your calendar? If so, then busy man, you've had a little day. Have you really ever thought of taking time to smell the flowers? I know, we're American workaholics; we don't like to do that. What we like to do is work. Play will come later, perhaps.

God knows that we can be consumed. He knows that He is the limitless one. So God has created a way for our burned-out situation to be brought to His limitless supply. You know what it is? God said there is a cycle in life — about one day in seven, everybody needs to stop. Did you hear that? One day in seven, we need to shut everything down and let the body and soul catch up with each other. The Jews took it literally. We were in Jerusalem on a Sabbath and it was shut down. But technologically-advanced America is burning itself out, because we won't stop. We have a holy day turned into a holiday.

God wants us to recreate ourselves inside, because we can be burned out. What you need is not a weekend in the mountains; you need a weekend in His Word, on your knees, in the place of God, worshiping to fill the inner man.

No wonder we get so burned out. Feeding the spirit is more than being a spectator once a month at a stadium event. Stop; turn aside to worship. When the Bible says, "Be still and know that I am God," that literally translated means, "Be quiet, so I can talk to you."

Prayer: *Sit quietly in a comfortable, relaxed position. Close your eyes and think of the most beautiful flower you've seen, or the loveliest, most tranquil place you know. Thank God for the beautiful things in your life . . . name some. Feel your soul calmed and at peace. Amen.*

BURNOUT

14. Trampling on Holy Ground

Exodus 3:1-7 *"Do not come any closer,"* God said. *"Take off your sandals, for the place where you are standing is holy ground." (v.5)*

The worship of God is high and holy. There is an awesome mystery about God. The whole book of Exodus, the whole Bible, reveals the ways of God to men. You don't learn "about" God; God "reveals" Himself to you. You don't find God; God finds you. What a scandal it is to think that we can know anything about God by our own initiative. God does the coming, and God came in the burning bush to Moses. He said it was holy. We, however, don't have a sense of the holy in our culture.

Several years ago, we went to the Masters golf tournament in Augusta, Georgia. Outside the gate, the crowd was like that at any athletic event — jubilant and noisy. But when the fans walked onto the course, it was as if they had walked onto holy ground. Many of them felt that they were having a holy experience, for this was where Bobby Jones and the greatest golfers of all times had been. People did not throw their cigarettes down and grind them into the ground; they carefully placed them in the proper containers. People arrived on time and stayed until it was over. If a player had trouble moving along, they stayed with him until he had completed his round. There was a sort of holy hush over the entire tournament.

The next day we returned to our church, where we had just completed a new sanctuary. People came late and left early. They ground their cigarettes into the turf of God. Where are we in America, we wondered, that the holy is in athletic contests and the profane is in the house of God? The sanctuary *is* the holy house of God. We come to worship the Lord God of all creation. We could claim, with the saints, that the Lord God Himself is among this body. A holy hush falls over the people. You don't judge the preaching; the Word of God judges us all. You don't judge the music; God speaks through the music to all of us. Take off your shoes — you're on holy ground.

Maybe you're burned out because your priorities are mixed up. Maybe you're burned out because you've been worshiping at the wrong altar. Maybe you're depleted because your sense of the holy has been out of focus. If you want your life right, you need to understand where it is, who He is. That's what it's all about. Any old bush will do, when God is burning.

Prayer: *Dear Father, remind me that all of life is sacred – Your place of worship and also the personalities of Your creation. Let me reverence all of life. Help me to be more kind and not to speak so harshly to these people (name them). Teach me the joys of worship in Your name. Amen.*

COMMITMENT

15. Anything, Lord, But Don't Ask Me To Sing in the Choir

Exodus 3:10-13 *"So now, go. I am sending you to Pharaoh to bring my people, the Israelites, out of Egypt." (v.10)*

Imagine this, if you can: An eighty-year-old escaped criminal, married to the daughter of a Bedouin sheik, is standing in the middle of the desert. He is called by God to go into what is probably the most powerful nation in the world to lead an enslaved people out of bondage. The idea seems totally impossible.

In the midst of this, we imagine that Moses was trying to decide if he really was hearing the voice of God, or if his imagination was playing tricks on him.

Can you imagine what it would be like to go down into that pagan world, to walk into the Pharaoh's court, and to tell him that you're going to take his slave labor force out of bondage and make them a new nation? Imagine how strange it would seem to walk among all of those Jewish people who were there working on the pyramids, and say to them, "God is calling me to take you out of bondage."

What would you have done? Moses could have been like many modern Americans. He could have stood back and said, "That's a good thing to do. Someone should do it." Moses could have said, "Lord, I have been having solitary communion with Thee out here in the desert for a long time, and I think it's good that those people will be freed from their bondage. Go find someone, or let me find someone for You, to go down there and lead them out." He could have said, like a modern American, "I think church is good. It's fine for people to drop in occasionally and make a contribution now and then. I'll do God a favor and show up once a month. I'll even come to the early service, and, if God is good enough to me, I'll come two Sundays in a row. I'll sit in the pew and sing a hymn. I'll put a dollar in the plate, but, God, don't ask me to do anything that hurts. Don't ask me to teach a class or be a deacon. Don't ask me to usher, or tithe, or sign a pledge card. And above all else, don't ask me to sing in the choir!"

As all the forces came together for Moses, the real issue became one of commitment. There comes a time for each person to face the real issues of life and determine his own commitment level. Are you ready to sing in the choir?

Prayer: *Heavenly Father, sometimes I don't know what You really want me to do. Help me to understand that the vague uneasiness I feel inside is Your way of showing me where my commitments should be. Keep me aware of Your voice, Your nudging me in your way. Let my life count for You today, especially in these areas (name some, like family and work relationships.) Amen.*

COMMITMENT

16. Who Am I, That I Should Go?

Exodus 3:10-14 *But Moses said to God, "Who am I, that I should go to Pharaoh and bring the Israelites out of Egypt?" (v.11)*

The question that Moses asked is quite simple — "Who am I?"

Everyone seems to be trying to find out who they are. We've looked in the mirror, like Narcissus, and we've fallen in love with ourselves. Nearly everyone is running around in circles, trying to find out who they are, where they've come from, and where they're going. And some of us are afraid that, if we ever do find ourselves, we'll look like our passport photos. The real struggle in life is not that we are looking *for* ourselves so much as we are running *from* ourselves.

Moses had to face up to that. God said to him, "I have a task for you to do." The thing you need to know is that you can't find a self apart from the one that God created.

The Bible teaches that we are made by God for a purpose. We didn't just happen. You cannot find yourself until you see how God made you to fit into His world.

Notice that Moses wasn't running around in the desert looking for God. He was tending sheep. He didn't say, "At last, I've found Him." He simply turned aside and saw the bush that burned. Over and over in the Bible, God does the coming. Moses didn't put an "I've Found It" sticker on his camel. You don't "find" God. Most of us, in fact, run and hide from God; but God comes.

God walked through the garden and called out for Adam and Eve, but they were hiding because they were naked. You know your sins, you know your guilt, but God does the coming. He finds you. And God's revelation of Himself to you is in direct proportion to the level of your commitment to Him.

Do you have a tired friendship with God and His church? If you do, you know it's actually not God's fault, or even the church's fault. It's more than likely your fault. You may have been taking your theology from the wrong trough, and you're getting indigestion. To really get to know God, you have to have commitment. That means praying, visiting, working in your church community. There's no such thing as a speculative jump into Christianity; it has to be a leap of faith, a real trust in the arms of God.

Prayer: *Dear Father, it is very difficult to pray for Your will to be done in my life. It is frightening to let You take complete control. Help me to be able to be still long enough to learn what You want me to be and to do. Amen.*

COMMITMENT

17. Who Are You?

Exodus 3:10-14 *Moses said to God, "Suppose I go to the Israelites and say to them, 'The God of your fathers has sent me to you,' and they ask me, 'What is his name?' Then what shall I tell them?" God said to Moses, "I am who I am. This is what you are to say to the Israelites: 'I AM has sent me to you.'"* (v.13,14)

Who are you? This was a question that had to be answered, yet God did a funny thing here. He didn't give Moses a direct answer. If you were Moses, wouldn't you want to know who you were representing? He could probably imagine Ramses II in gold armament, sitting on his throne with courtiers around him. Moses, this weary, weather-beaten old shepherd, could imagine what it would be like, standing there saying to Ramses, "God sent me down here." Surely everyone would laugh.

So Moses asked, "What's your name, God? Which name fits You? They have the god of the sun, and the god of the Nile, the god of the crops, the god of fertility, and all of these other gods around here, and when I walk in, I want to be able to show them some credentials." God gave him this riddle: "I Am who I Am." What kind of answer is that? Imagine standing before Pharaoh and all the slaves and saying, "Some guy by the name of 'I AM' sent me down here to take you out of bondage." You probably wouldn't get very far.

Let's look at the name. In the Hebrew language, running two words together that way — I am who I am — reinforces the meaning. It's more than plural. It could mean perfection, but there is more to it than that. The verb is "to be." Why did God use this? Because the verb "to be" is open-ended; it's moving. He is saying that He is the God who is bigger than any human name, a perfect God. God will not be categorized by us. God will not be pressed into some kind of little mold or tag.

Any time we put a label on something, we've limited it. If we say God is love, that's good, but it's not enough. He's more than love. If we say that He is righteous, that's good, but He is more than righteous. The Bible does not play around with petty understandings of God. The Lord God, who is beyond our categories, speaks to us, and we cannot comprehend. But it is clear that He wants our total allegiance and commitment.

Prayer: *Dear Father, how great You are. My vocabulary is too limited, my mind too small, to ever understand You completely. I want to grow and learn about You. Help me to open my mind and heart, and not squelch new ideas that make me think. Thank You for the people You have placed in my life to direct and suggest areas of learning. (Pray for these people by name: your pastor, church leaders, your Sunday school teacher, and others who teach. Remember that those who teach and preach God's word will be held accountable to God Himself. Always pray for them.) Amen.*

COMMITMENT

18. Who Are They?

Exodus 3:16 *"Go, assemble the elders of Israel and say to them, 'The Lord, the God of your fathers, the God of Abraham, Isaac and Jacob, appeared to me and said: I have watched over you and have seen what has been done to you in Egypt.'"*

Who are these people whom Moses has to lead? He is to go to the elders, the leaders of Israel, and enlist their support. Moses didn't have to work alone. Also note that when the Exodus began, it was not just one or two people ready to tramp through the desert, but a whole nation. There was no individualism here. They all had to work and move on the same schedule. If the time of departure didn't fit the needs of one family, they just had to conform in order to receive the comfort and protection of the group.

If your commitment is real, you need a community of faith around you. There is a singleness of heart that floats around America, saying, "All I need is Jesus and me." This is not true. Jesus had twelve people around Him, and around that twelve were one hundred and twenty, and around them were another five hundred. The Bible doesn't know anything about this individualism that we see in America. We float around thinking an "experience" with Jesus is all we need. It will die! You don't convert a man and send him out into the street, anymore than you take a baby out into the parking lot and watch him walk home.

"Upon this rock, I will build my church." Jesus organized a church. He never intended for us to float around by ourselves and pop in here and there. He intends for you to be in a community that will limit your excesses, keep you from being too extreme, and pick you up when you're sagging. You're not made to be alone. You can't have one finger; you have to have a hand. You can't have an arm without a body. We're just parts that must come together to form the body of Christ. Many people are dying spiritually, because they have never faced up to the fact that they must take on the responsibility of a community of faith. You need a family around you; you can't live in isolation. Some of you don't want that kind of commitment — you're afraid of it. You want the fruit of it, you want the joy of it, you want the good parts of it, but you don't want that kind of commitment.

23

Until you are ready to express that commitment — the choir, the class, the group — there is no burning bush.

Prayer: *Thank You, dear Father, for the community of faith that holds me close to You. Show me new ways of "pulling my load." Let me be more aware of the hurts, the disappointments, the needs of others, and to reach out to them. (Think of people you know who are distressed, and pray for them by name.) Amen.*

YOU'LL PAY FOR THIS

19. The Price of Freedom

Exodus 8:25 *Then Pharaoh summoned Moses and Aaron and said, "Go, sacrifice to your God here in the land."*

Moses had finally gotten in to see Pharaoh and requested, "Let my people go," but Pharaoh refused. He made the workload even heavier on the Hebrews, so they would be angry and blame Moses for their distress.

Moses went back to Pharaoh and, again, was refused. Then the plagues came — plagues of frogs, of flies, of lice — and Pharaoh had to rethink his decision. Old Pharaoh was not dumb. He said to Moses, "You can take a week off to worship your God right here. You don't need to go into the desert. You just stay here and worship your God. I don't know who He is, but I'm willing to let your people worship Him for a week right here."

That is not what God had asked for. God said, "I want my people to be free."

Are you in bondage? The minute the Lord God begins to say to you that you must come out, you can be sure that the Pharaoh in your life becomes more oppressive. When the power of God comes to liberate people who are held in bondage, the power of evil gets tough. If we learn anything in the Bible, it is that evil does not let go easily. You may be held in bondage, and you may think that somehow you can slither away from that Pharaoh. Then he says, "Don't become a Christian; don't get all involved in church; don't let God get too deep into your life. Just think good religious thoughts where you are. Don't move; stay where you are. You don't have to give up illicit sex, excessive alcohol, your bad attitude; you don't have to do any of these things to be a Christian. You don't even have to go to church." That's Pharaoh talking.

There are many people in this kind of situation. They have good jobs, making good money. Then someone from the community of God invites them to come out of the bondage of secularism, and to be with the people of God. They reply, "No, we want a little religion and we'll come by, but don't ask us to give; don't ask us to put our lives there. We don't want to leave what we have." But you don't get anything unless you leave something.

Moses wouldn't agree to Pharaoh's offer. Three more plagues came — boils, hail, and fire. Pharaoh's heart was hard, because he was fighting with God. It's not easy to come out of bondage, and it's not easy to get people out. A contest was going on, and Pharaoh was determined to keep those people in bondage.

Prayer: *Father, I am in bondage, but I want to be free. Help me shed the shackles that keep me from all You want me to be. Help me to overcome (name your areas of bondage). In Jesus' name. Amen.*

YOU'LL PAY FOR THIS

20. A Little Religion

Exodus 8:28 *Pharaoh said, "I will let you go to offer sacrifices to the Lord your God in the desert, but you must not go very far. Now pray for me."*

Pharaoh said, "I was wrong when I said stay here. I know you want to go out into the Sinai desert. That's not the greatest place in the world, but if that's what you want to do, then go." What he was really saying was, "You go, but don't go very far." That's the second compromise Pharaoh gave Moses, and it's the second compromise the power of evil gives to you. The Pharaoh in your life is saying, "Go to church, be a Christian, join Sunday School, and go once a year. That's O.K., but don't go very far." Some of you have listened to Pharaoh and learned that, if you give in just a little bit, you'll satisfy everybody who is pushing; you'll satisfy a little bit of your conscience, and you'll satisfy Pharaoh. And you wonder why you're unhappy with your Christian commitment?

You really are frightened of becoming a religious fanatic, aren't you? You've seen some friends who went off the deep end on religion, and you don't want that to happen to you. Of course, a man will get up at three in the morning to drive four hours to get to a fishing place when the sun comes up. But we don't want any fanaticism in our religion. We worship these false gods and say to the Lord God of the universe, "You just come and make it a little better for us, make us look good, but don't get into our lives."

Do you ever wonder why there is nothing in reserve when you need it? It's because there has been no investment. That's where most of the people are. For those of you who are just halfway in, who left a little bit of Egypt behind but don't really want much of Sinai, there will never be any happiness or fulfillment in your life, as long as you hang back.

Prayer: *Dear Father, I want to be on better terms with You. I'd like to be able to feel comfortable in Your presence. Give me the courage to be open to Your guidance and to be involved in Your work. Let me feel the warmth and freedom in Your love. Amen.*

YOU'LL PAY FOR THIS

21. Sacrifice Your Children

Exodus 10: 8-11 *"No! Have only the men go; and worship the Lord, since that's what you have been asking for." (v.11)*

Once again, Pharaoh called Moses in. "You can go worship, but while you're out there, I want you to leave your women and children here." That was a pretty good deal. They could go as far as they wanted, but they were to leave their children in Egypt.

Communist countries give visas to travel outside the country, but the traveler's family is left behind. Some of you have done the same thing. The eighth verse of the tenth chapter talks about that.

We used to live in a culture that reinforced the family. You turned on the radio, and the hero always won. You knew that what was taught in school and what your children saw on the newsstand would support your family.

That day is gone. You think you're living in a Christian America, but you're not. That day is gone. The law says we can't give you that kind of support at school. Dollars say we can't get that support from the community, because there is too much money being made tearing up the home. That leaves the community of faith as the only place that supports the family. I've seen too many parents who have said, "Wait a minute, I want all the secular values in my house, but I don't want any faith. Let the church do something."

God said, you come with your family and invest your lives here and put your roots here, and, together, we'll build that family. You can't go in a little way and leave your children behind.

Is your family committed? Are you all together? When problems do come to your family (and they will), it's a good feeling to know that you have made sure your children have experienced the warmth of a family of faith, the security of a loving God, and the examples of strong men and women. The community of faith offers resources for living in a precarious day.

Prayer: *Father, bless our homes. Bless the home in which I live. (Name those in your family.) Help me to be a good family participant, doing my part to make us aware of Your undeserved love. Amen.*

YOU'LL PAY FOR THIS

22. Sacrifice Your Wealth

Exodus 10:20-26 *". . . Go, worship the Lord. Even your women and children may go with you; only leave your flocks and herds behind." (v.24)*

Pharaoh called Moses in and said, "Go; I'm tired of you. But I want you to leave your wealth behind." The Hebrews had been successful merchants, shepherds, and carpenters. They were a wealthy people, before the Pharaoh made slaves of them. "Go, but leave your wealth here," is an insidious remark, isn't it?

A lot of us have done the same thing with our lives. God called us to join His church, to be a part of His kingdom, but we left our possessions behind. He wants all of us.

Moses refused to leave without the wealth of his people. They needed the animals and jewelry for worship. It was important then, and it is equally important today, that we worship God with our tithes and offerings. On the first day of the week, we are to take our tithes and offerings to the church. Take a note from Moses: Move out of Pharaoh's territory lock, stock, and barrel.

Prayer: *Father, thank You for teaching us how to become free from the slavery to Pharaoh. Give us the courage to leave the bondage and become all that You created us to be. Amen.*

HOW DARK THE NIGHT

23. Darkness That Can Be Felt

Exodus 10:21 *Then the Lord said to Moses, "Stretch out your hand toward the sky so that darkness will spread over Egypt – darkness that can be felt."*

In Philadelphia several years ago, a court ruled a man sane in the daytime and insane at night. The judgment seems strange, but a lot of people live that way. They are very sane during the day, working hard to take care of their families, paying their taxes, and obeying the law. But when night comes, they throw it all away. They spend their days compensating for the insanity of their nights.

Look through the Bible and you'll find that many empires were lost by night. Belshazzar lost his kingdom at night, and all the sins of his darkness came crashing down on his day. Like him, we become shackled by the sins of our darkness.

In 1759, the British and the French were fighting over the treasures of the Americas. On a September night of that year, the British gathered their forces and marched to a place called Abraham. They took their boats across the St. Lawrence River and set up camp in such a way that, when dawn came, they would be ready. Guns were in place, bayonets were fixed, and all their lines were properly supplied. At dawn, battle ensued. The French and English fought all day. The British began to win, not because of their superior weapons, but because they had paid the price the night before to get in place.

Some men lose themselves in the nighttime; others gain victory. Darkness seems to harbor all kinds of fear in our hearts. You feel it when you're peering from the window for the lights of your teen-ager's car. Darkness can be felt when you're pacing the floor of the intensive care unit of the hospital, waiting to hear the condition of your loved one.

Remember that darkness is familiar to everyone. The important thing is that the darkness will not swallow us, because God is walking with us every step of the way, no matter what happens. God gained the victory for mankind in the nighttime.

Prayer: *O Lord, I pray with the Psalmist: "Deliver me from evil men. Preserve me from the violent, who plot and stir up trouble all day long. Their words sting like poisonous snakes. Keep me out of their power. Preserve me from their violence . . . Let me live in your presence." Amen.*

HOW DARK THE NIGHT

24. Cries in the Night

Exodus 11:4 *This is what the Lord says: "About midnight, I will go throughout Egypt."*
Exodus 11:6 *"There will be loud wailing throughout Egypt – worse than there has ever been or ever will be again."*

Four thousand years ago, the battle was raging between Moses and Pharaoh over the slavery of the Hebrew people in Egypt. Nine plagues were brought upon old Pharaoh. Then that great struggle came to set the people free. Moses stood before Pharaoh and warned him, then he went back to the camp of the Hebrews to tell them that the tenth plague would be different. It would be visited upon everyone.

You know the story. They were to go and get a four-day-old lamb and bring it into the home, so that it would become a part of the family. This lamb was to be killed ceremoniously, and the blood spread over the door where everyone could see it. Then, on that dark night in history, the Death Angel, God Himself, would move across the land. The firstborn in any home that did not have blood over the door would be killed. Remember that God was just. He provided a way for everybody in Egypt — Hebrew and Egyptian — to be saved from the Death Angel. The firstborn in Biblical times represented prosperity and hope for the family. Everything centered around the firstborn.

Then that night came. It was the darkest night of history, for this was the night that the back of evil was to be broken. This was the night that the salvation of the world was to be foreshadowed. This was the night that God had planned, since the foundation of the earth, to bring men out of bondage. God had shown to all men that the death of human sin is greater than we could have imagined, and this night it was made clear.

God went in the form of the Death Angel, and you could hear the cries around the city. Where there was no blood over the door, a baby died. Again and again, babies of Egypt died. You could hear the wailing of the mothers in the night, as they got up and cried out over the deaths of their children. The Hebrews crouched in the corners of their homes, listening to the crying of the Egyptians. They knew God was moving the tenth plague over the city. They knew that they also could be struck down. The Death Angel came over the place where

31

the Hebrews were encamped, and not a Hebrew family with blood over the lintel of the door was struck. The Hebrew mothers were crying with joy, and the fathers were happy that they had listened to what Moses and Aaron had said.

Prayer: *Thank You, Father, for providing a way out of the darkness. Thank You for hearing the wails of the brokenhearted. Let me be obedient and faithful. Teach me Your ways. Amen.*

HOW DARK THE NIGHT

25. Skeptics and the Darkness

Exodus 12:12 *"On that same night, I will pass through Egypt . . . and I will bring judgment on all the gods of Egypt. I am the Lord."*

Skeptics always seem to expect God to make special accommodations for them, and they are indignant when this is not the case. The skeptics that night in Egypt learned that there is only one way out of the land of bondage.

A skeptic, who didn't like Moses and was jealous of his education and his escape from hard work, questioned his wisdom. Moses said to slay the lamb, but the Hebrew skeptic said, "Not me; I know more than he does. Moses thinks he's smart, because he's been out in the Sinai desert, but I'm as smart as he is."

So this Hebrew skeptic didn't get a lamb and didn't put the blood over his door. He said, "I have a good family background. I'm a son of Abraham. God won't do anything to me. I've been good all my life. I've kept all of the regulations that have been given to us. When that Death Angel comes over, God will look down and see my righteousness and I'll be O.K." But there is no provision for the goodness of anyone. There is no provision for family, work, or righteousness. The only provision was the blood of the lamb over the door. God said do it this way, but the skeptic said, "I know better." It cost him his firstborn.

You may be chained to sin, but God has made a way for you to get out. You may stand back and laugh about the bloody sacrifice and the blood over the door, but there is only one way, and that is through the blood of the Lord Jesus Christ.

The New Testament is filled with the identification of Jesus as the Lamb. Jesus is God's lamb, slain for you before the foundation of the earth. You can come out of bondage, but it won't be because you're good or brilliant. It won't be because of what your father or anyone else has done. It will be because of Jesus Christ. You have the option of taking that blood for yourself, or denying it.

The atonement is complete. It's interesting that people are always trying to see the atonement as being incomplete. They say that you must work for salvation. No. You cannot work yourself into the Kingdom. It is done there, and it is done for all. The merit of the blood is ours, and it can be yours through faith and trust in the lamb of God.

Prayer: *O Lord, I pray that You will remove my skepticism and sophistication, so that I may see the wonder of the love You have for Your children. Thank you for providing me with a way out of bondage, and for making it so simple. Help me to trust You completely in the darkness of my night. Amen.*

HOW DARK THE NIGHT

26. What "If?"

Exodus 12:31 *During the night, Pharaoh summoned Moses and Aaron and said, "Up! Leave my people, you and the Israelites! Go, worship the Lord as you have requested."*

After all the terror that had taken place in the darkness, the Hebrews finally got good news during the night. They began gathering their worldly possessions together. It was a rather comic scene: One hundred thousand men, plus women, children, and servants, camels, donkeys, and baggage, all moving toward freedom.

Can you imagine the excitement of these people? God had finally started them on their way to freedom. Yet, I'm sure there was terror in the hearts of many of the people. Women who were heavy in pregnancy worried about where their babies would be born. The old men and women were afraid they would get sick and be a hindrance to the family. The women called to their children to stay close by. The middle-aged men began to wonder aloud if Moses really had understood God correctly. After all, they were taking a strange route. Excitement and terror ran equally high, and this strange group began to move out of the bondage of Egypt, toward freedom.

Sometimes it's hard for us to decipher the messages we receive at night. Darkness makes us receive even good news with "what ifs" flying around our heads. We've had bad news for so long that good news is hard to handle. The security of captivity is difficult to leave, when faced with the unknown of freedom. We know how to maneuver in slavery, but it requires work to acquire new skills for freedom.

Prayer: *We do pray for our freedom, Heavenly Father. We also pray for the ability to handle good news and success. Give me freedom from the terror that lurks near every new opportunity. Amen.*

HOW DARK THE NIGHT

27. Remember This

Exodus 12:42 *Because the Lord kept vigil that night to bring them out of Egypt, on this night all the Israelites are to keep vigil to honor the Lord for generations to come.*

Think of some of the important events of your life — a special birthday celebration, the birth of a brother or sister, the death of a family member, your wedding day, your baptism, the big promotion, your son's arrest (or your arrest), committing your loved one to a drug/alcohol hospital, the birth of a grandchild. We could go on and on. Some things never fade entirely from our memories. As you bring these memories forward, talk to God about each one. If you have questions, ask him. Thank him for the happy ones, and for strength to have endured the unhappy ones.

The children of Israel were instructed to always celebrate the night of deliverance. We also must celebrate the nights of God's vigilance in our lives. He is dependable, and we should celebrate that frequently. His order to the Israelites was "to keep vigil," and so must we.

Prayer: *Our prayer today will be that of the Psalmist: "Because the Lord is my shepherd, I have everything I need! He lets me rest in the meadow grass and leads me beside the quiet streams. He restores my failing health. He helps me do what honors him the most. Even when walking through the dark valley of death, I will not be afraid, for You are close beside me, guarding, guiding all the way. You provide delicious food for me in the presence of mine enemies. You have welcomed me as Your guest; blessings overflow! Your goodness and unfailing kindness shall be with me all of my life, and afterwards I will live with You forever in Your home." Amen. (The Living Bible)*

READY FOR TRAVEL

28. Where Are You Headed?

Exodus 13:17 *When Pharoah let the people go, God did not lead them on the road through the Philistine country, though that was shorter. For God said, "If they face war, they might change their minds and return to Egypt."*

It would seem logical that anyone leading this many people out of bondage should take the quickest route possible. But God, in his wisdom, told Moses not to go that way. Why not? The shortest route would be northeast by the coast of Philistra, then across the top of the Sinai peninsula, and into the Promised Land. However, this was the military trail. The Egyptians had fortifications all along there. Can't you imagine this group walking by these fortifications? It would scare them to death. They had learned to bow down to the Egyptian. They knew what the whip of the Egyptian was like. Looking up at these forts as they went by would be too much for them.

Also, they weren't ready. They were new to freedom. They knew what it was like to be hemmed in, beaten down, and told what to do, but they didn't know what it was like to make up their own minds. They didn't have enough religion to survive. They were not yet a nation. So when you look at the map of the Exodus, you see that they went almost due south, then crossed over the sea, and went down into the southern part of the Sinai Peninsula.

Did God call you long ago? Did you try to plan your life accordingly? You knew where you were going and what you wanted to be. You wanted to make your life amount to something. But God didn't lead you that way. You saw a Promised Land out there and started in that direction, but God led you another way.

Where is God in all of this? We often think that the shortest distance between two points is a straight line. But in the mind of God, it isn't. We live in an "instant" generation: Put in a quarter and get a Coke out of a vending machine; turn on a switch and a light comes on. But God is not an "instant" God. God is more concerned about developing people than He is about doing things on our timetable. Personality, spirituality, commitment, and maturation don't come instantly.

God knew that if he had taken His people into the Promised Land that day, they could not have made it. They would have been killed. They could have been in the Promised Land in about thirty days, but it took them forty years to get there, because they needed to harden into a nation.

Now what about you? God is doing something with you. Everytime the Israelites camped or wandered, God was with them, directing them. Are you mad at God because He didn't let you do it your way? Are you angry because He turned you in another direction? Are you disillusioned because there is a blemish on your life? None of us is immune from life. God uses the circuitous routes to season and prepare us for life. God has something for each of us, but we can't get there by trying to find a shortcut. We have to go through the wilderness in order to be tough and ready for the Promised Land.

Prayer: *Think about some of the unexpected turns your life has taken. Remember that God has provided for you at each turn, however painful it was. Thank Him for His eternal, caring presence in your life. Amen.*

READY FOR TRAVEL

29. Who Is Going Along?

Exodus 12:38 *Many other people went up with them, as well as large droves of livestock, both flocks and herds.*

We usually think that everyone who came out of bondage was a Hebrew. The Bible says they were a "mixed multitude." When you have a parade of about a million people, you're bound to have a lot of people following along. They had robbers, scoundrels, debtors, malcontents, and misfits join them. And remember, the Hebrews didn't go poor. They had gone to their friends and called in their debts. They had picked up the valuables buried in their tents, and they had all the wealth they could manage with them. This obviously would tempt many people to go along.

Remember the story Jesus told about the man who went fishing? He threw in his net and, when he pulled it out, he didn't have all trout. He got a lot of different kinds of fish. The ones that were no good, he threw out. Jesus also talked about a man sowing the grain. He threw it out into the field and, when it came up, there were weeds, too. The same soil that produced the fruit also produced the weeds.

Now, you must understand that the church isn't perfect. The children of God are not perfect. The problem is with the mixed multitude; it's difficult to take the tares away from the wheat. But we don't want to tear up the field and throw away the crop, just to get rid of a few weeds.

These people who tagged along with the Hebrews probably said things like, "Moses is just on an ego trip. He's the biggest immigrator in the world. If he had any sense, he would go the other way. Who wants to worship that invisible God of his, anyway?" Perhaps you've been tagging along, hanging around the edges of the church. Have you been enjoying the nourishment without the commitment? Do you want to hitch a ride and enjoy the trip without having any responsibility?

The point is that there was mixed baggage that went along with the people of Israel. We'll never be free of it, and our only defense is to know where we're going and not be diverted. We're going to God's Promised Land.

Prayer: *Heavenly Father, thank You for the church and Your people, who are striving to move forward to the Promised Land. Let me never be a stumbling block. Let me be faithful to follow Your guidance. Now, today, help me to be a blessing to someone in need. Make me sensitive to the needs of others. Amen.*

READY FOR TRAVEL

30. What Are You Taking?

Exodus 13:19 *Moses took the bones of Joseph with him, because Joseph had made the sons of Israel swear an oath. He had said, "God will surely come to your aid, and then you must carry my bones up with you from this place."*

On your journey to the Promised Land, what are you taking along? A lot of people try to go through life without any baggage at all. Moses probably thought that he had enough to worry about, but he kept the promise made to Joseph. You remember that Joseph had been sold into slavery in Egypt, but his heart always yearned to return home. Before he died, he called his brothers to him and made them swear to take his bones when they left Egypt. He was embalmed and placed in a coffin in Egypt (Gen. 50:26). Joseph had passed on the promise that God would come to their aid. What kind of promise are you passing on to the people in your house?

Many of us have enjoyed the advantage of having Godly parents and grandparents, who have passed on their religious heritage and made it possible for us to enjoy a personal religious experience. That experience has carried us through the death of a spouse or the rebellion of a child, and we acknowledge that, without our faith and trust in God, we never could have made it. However, we fail to give our children the opportunity to experience the very things that have held us together in hard times. It is as though we have the right to ignore our heritage and background, because God didn't take us the direct route to our Promised Land. God does keep His promises, and we must take that with us always and pass it on to others.

Prayer: *Father, forgive me for failing to pass on Your great promises – my heritage. Give me courage and wisdom to carry on today, to be aware of human need, and to be available to help others. Amen.*

41

READY FOR TRAVEL

31. Who Is Your Leader?

Exodus 13:21-22 By day, the Lord went ahead of them in a pillar of cloud to guide them on their way, and by night in a pillar of fire to give them light, so that they could travel by day or night. Neither the pillar of cloud by day or the pillar of fire by night left its place in front of the people.

A long time ago, there was a man who spent some time with a caravan in the Sinai desert. He said that the caravan was being organized so that people would not be lost. At the front, there would be men with big torches and charcoal braziers, that would give off smoke. The caravan might be several miles long, and the smoke would come back over the route, so that the ones in the middle would know where the head of the caravan was. If the sun was very hot and they had to travel at night, they could see the light from the torches.

Are you on a long pilgrimage out in a wilderness? You've been through death, through depression; you're in the wilderness of doubt and don't know whether you're going to make it. You're looking at your life and saying, "Is this all there is? Has God abandoned me out here? Will I ever find my way into the Promised Land? Where is God in the midst of all of this?" The Scriptures tell us very clearly that God always has his pillar of cloud over us, and this is the symbol of the presence of God. God has not abandoned his people. Whatever you're facing, remember it's the devil's word that says, "You've had problems, God has abandoned you." God says, "I am with you." Jesus' name is Immanuel and that means, "God with us." "Lo, I am with you always, even until the end of the age." "Though I walk through the valley of the shadow of death, I will fear no evil, for Thou art with me."

Everything in Hebrew life was interpreted as being a sign from God. So the Jews took this as a symbol from God that He would be with them all the time. There would be the light at the head of the caravan that God used to guide them. The man back in the middle of the caravan would know that five miles ahead, in this long procession, was a man who was carrying the torch, and that he was under the leadership of God. At night he would know that the small dot of light was the vanguard of the group, and that God was leading. In your wilderness, it may seem like an aimless journey, but the hand of

God is in it. The ages, the angels, and the enternities are set to lead God's people.

Prayer: *"O Lord, hear my prayer; listen to my cry for mercy; in Your faithfulness and righteousness, come to my relief."*

"For Your name's sake, O Lord, preserve my life: in Your righteousness, bring me out of trouble." (Psalm 143:1,11) Thank You, O Lord, for Your unspeakable mercy and love. Amen.

BETWEEN THE DEVIL AND THE DEEP RED SEA

32. Caught in the Middle

Exodus 14:2b,10 *They are to encamp by the sea, directly opposite Baal Zephon . . . As Pharaoh approached, the Israelites looked up, and there were the Egyptians, marching after them. They were terrified and cried out to the Lord.*

The parting of the Red Sea is perhaps the most vivid account in the life of Israel. It is to the Jews what the resurrection is to the Christian church. One of the most graphic pictures in the Old Testament is the contrast coming together here. This is *the* paramount contrast. God never plays with winners, always with losers. Every time God tells us about strength in the Scriptures, we see how weak it is. You have little David winning against Goliath, and now you have the pitiful group of Israelites coming out of bondage, facing Pharaoh's army.

Can't you imagine what they looked like, with camels and horses, dogs and cats, and all the extended families? They were a frightened, unorganized people as they came to the Red Sea. They didn't know what they were going to do. To understand all the symbolism here, you have to understand that the Hebrews never liked the water at all. The seas were a symbol of chaos for them. They never became great seafarers. Even in the times of Solomon, when they had their own navy, they employed the seafaring Philistines to go out in their ships. Now they were faced with a great problem. They had before them the chaos of the Red Sea, and they had behind them the Egyptian army. You can be sure that Pharaoh was doing all he could to get them back into bondage. He had been humiliated by Moses and the ten plagues; he had been through a disaster when all the firstborn of the Egyptians had been killed; and in reaction to all of that, Pharaoh changed his mind about letting them go. The people of God were caught in the middle.

Being caught in the middle makes you feel stranded. We can get caught between friends who are quarreling or between our parents. We sometimes are caught between our children and real-life experiences that may hurt. Some people are crushed between the generations. Have you ever been caught in the middle and been made a messenger for the two parties? Being in the middle can be frightening, however you experience it. We need to learn to be supportive of both sides, but we also need to let them work it out. Learn appropriate ways to let others take responsibility for their own actions and situations. That's the best thing you can do for them.

Prayer: *Dear Father, give me courage to remove myself from grinding situations. Help me to give encouragement to others, but to allow them the privilege of accepting the responsibility for their lives. Father, there are some situations that cannot be removed just now, and I pray for sound judgment, an open mind and heart, and a sweet spirit. Amen.*

BETWEEN THE DEVIL AND THE DEEP RED SEA

33. Symbol of Evil

Exodus 14:5 *When the king of Egypt was told that the people had fled, Pharaoh and his officials changed their minds about them and said, "What have we done? We have let the Israelites go and have lost their services."*

Pharaoh is the symbol of evil in this story, and you must understand that evil in the Bible is never underestimated. It's only modern man who underestimates evil. We have a rather careless view of it. We haven't really come to grips with how strong evil is in our culture. When someone comes out of the bondage of sin and makes a profession of faith, he thinks that's all there is to it. No more problems. From now on, it's going to be easy. That's modern American Christianity, but it isn't the Bible's Christianity.

Do you remember when Jesus was up on the mount being tempted? The devil came to him and tempted him very strongly. When the temptations were over and Jesus had withstood them, the devil departed promising to come again at another time. Never are we free from the pressures, the temptations, the fear, and the antagonism of evil. The Bible says it is not enough just to be liberated; we need to come out of bondage and then do away with the problem. These people would never be free until Pharaoh was dead.

We are always tempted to make excuses for our unpleasant situations. Perhaps you have an unhappy marriage, bad working conditions, or live in an undesirable neighborhood. You like to think that a change would transform everything in your life. But we have to learn to deal with whatever we're in and face up to the situation. Perhaps the change needs to be deep within ourselves — a bad attitude, poor health or work habits, a frightening temper, or a hidden (you think) addiction.

The main lesson of the Bible is that weakness in God always triumphs over strength in the devil. God's weakness is always more powerful than the devil's strength. According to the Bible, the mustard seed is much more powerful than anyone thinks it is. What you need to understand today is that Pharaoh's army cannot take you captive again. God will not let him come and take you captive again, unless you lay down your arms, quit fighting, and go back into captivity voluntarily.

46

Prayer: *Father, thank You for giving us Your strength and power during hard times. Let me not forget the main lesson of the Bible – that You are always with us. Amen.*

BETWEEN THE DEVIL AND THE DEEP RED SEA

34. We Told You So

Exodus 14:11,12 *They said to Moses, "Was it because there were no graves in Egypt that you brought us to the desert to die? What have you done to us by bringing us out of Egypt? Didn't we say to you in Egypt, 'Leave us alone; let us serve the Egyptians?'"*

There is a theme that goes through the book of Exodus — "We don't want to do this." They wanted to get out of bondage, but they didn't want the journey to the Promised Land. These were people of very little faith. When God went to get a chosen people, He looked down not at Rome or Jerusalem, but at Egypt. He found some slaves and said, "You're chosen." Their response was, "We don't want to be chosen." But God chose them anyway. And in the whole process, they didn't think God was big enough to take care of their problems. Their memories were so short. They had forgotten how God had prevailed during the ten plagues, how God had given Moses the vision, how God had humbled Pharaoh. Their lack of faith brought sarcasm. "Moses, there comes Pharaoh, here is the sea, what are you going to do?" Then that remark, "Aren't there enough graves in Egypt, without you bringing us out here to die?"

You can hear those "I told you so's" now. A critic never builds anything; he's just an authority on tearing down what other people have built. A constructive critic gets his shoulder to the wheel and works with you, but this kind of critic doesn't. He's an authority at telling you it can't be done. Theodore Roosevelt said, "I don't mind you criticizing my administration, if you'll get down here and help me do the job, but if you're just going to stand there in the bleachers while we do the work, you have no right to criticize."

We have critics all around us, but God is always there giving faith to His leaders. Security is something you have to give up when you go with God, because He doesn't play with the security of the world. He plays with the security that comes from the other world, from the mind and heart of the eternities. When you face your critics, remember that only those who see the vision and take their marching orders from the Lord God are the ones who accomplish anything.

Prayer: *Father, please deliver me from being faithless; deliver me to faithfulness. Let me be supportive of Your work. Amen.*

BETWEEN THE DEVIL AND THE DEEP RED SEA

35. Pattern for Leadership

Exodus 14:13 *Moses answered the people, "Do not be afraid. Stand firm and you will see the deliverance the Lord will bring you today. The Egyptians you see today you will never see again."*

Moses was a man of faith. He was in a situation that called for remarkable leadership. Perhaps you can identify with his plight. Before you is chaos; behind you are the forces of evil. The people you're leading want to know why you don't just go back and die. There was no consensus anywhere in the whole process, so Moses went away from the people and started talking to God. We imagine he had quite a few questions to ask God. And what did God say? God told Moses it was time to stop praying and begin acting. God told him to prepare the people to move forward.

In the life of Israel, this is the resurrection. It doesn't matter how God delivers us; the important thing is that He does deliver us. Modern man wants to look at every piece of wiring, every brick in a building, to be sure it's in the right place. That isn't the way of faith.

God told Moses what to do. Those words, "Fear not, stand still, see the salvation of the Lord," simply mean to let God do His thing.

The Bible tells us that there was an east wind blowing all night. The symbolism is overwhelming. The west wind normally brought clouds in off the sea, which meant rain. It was a calming wind that boosted agricultural production. The east wind blew in off the desert, and it always brought a change in things. The Scriptures tell us that all night long the east wind blew. Then, when in the providence of God, the wind blew so strong and hard that the walls of water went back, and the people of Israel went forward. Nowhere in the Bible does God send His people back.

The only time they went back was when they appointed a committee, and it didn't do what God wanted it to do. The committee saw the giants and wandered until that generation died. God always sends His people forward. The people of God go forward with the blessing of God. When they opt to go backward, they opt for punishment. Forward is the watchword of the Bible.

Prayer: *Dear Father, thank You for leaders who are faithful and stand firm in times of stress. Give us strength to go forward, whatever the cost may be. Make us people of faith. Amen.*

BETWEEN THE DEVIL AND THE DEEP RED SEA

36. Symbols of Victory

Exodus 14:30 *That day the Lord saved Israel from the hands of the Egyptians, and Israel saw the Egyptians lying dead on the shore.*

After they had made it across and the water had come back down, they looked on the shores and saw the remains of the Egyptian army. Imagine their walking along the shores, looking at the evidence of God's deliverance. God gives us the victory and the symbols of victory.

Look at your past. Where have you been held captive? Have you made your exodus? God provides for us in our times of bondage; He never leaves us alone. He provides ways of escape and encourages us to use them. Then He gives the evidence of your deliverance — the dead Egyptians along the shore. What bonds are holding you captive? Are you paralyzed by fears — fear of failure, fear of rejection, fear of the future, fear of being committed to God? Had you rather be back in Egypt in slavery than make the effort and commitment to be free? That's what the children of Israel had to decide. They would have returned to slavery and never experienced the joys of victory.

Life is a pilgrimage from slavery to the Promised Land. It is a constant progression, with obstacles and evils along the way, but it can be done with the presence of God. Look back over your shoulder at the dead Egyptians, the symbols of victory. See the loneliness, fear, despair, doubt, anxiety, and desolation lying along your shore? You're in bondage no longer!

Prayer: *"The Lord is my strength and my song; He has become my salvation. He is my God, and I will praise Him."*

"In your unfailing love, you will lead the people you have redeemed. In your strength, you will guide them to your holy dwelling."

"The Lord will reign forever." Exodus 15:2,13,18

SOMETIMES I'M UP, SOMETIMES I'M DOWN

37. Celebration

Exodus 15:19,20 *When Pharaoh's horses, chariots, and horsemen went into the sea, the Lord brought the waters of the sea back over them, but the Israelites walked through the sea on dry ground. Then Miriam, the prophetess, Aaron's sister, took a tambourine in her hand, and all the women followed her, with tambourines and dancing.*

Celebration is a good thing. There are times when you just need to celebrate. The Israelites were at such a time. God had delivered them, had opened the Red Sea for them. They couldn't believe it was happening. When they thought they were going to die, they were delivered. Then the sea closed up and killed all of Pharaoh's soldiers. They broke into an absolute celebration. Can't you just imagine how Moses felt? Many times we feel crushed by life, and then things are right again and there is an overwhelming sense of God's celebration in us.

The church has always been a place of celebration. At Easter we celebrate the salvation of mankind through the breaking of the chains of death at the tomb. We come together on the first day of the week. The significant moments of celebration are the key events in the life of the church. At Christmas we celebrate that God invaded history and delivered men from the chains of the evil one. Many people want celebration to be the whole of the Christian faith, but the Bible doesn't let us stay on the shore of the Red Sea in constant revelry.

The Israelites thought they were coming out of bondage to an instant Promised Land. We've brought up generation after generation of people, and we've misled them by implication. We've made people think that all they have to do is take that step, cross through the waters, and, when they step on the other side, all is celebration and sweetness in life. Don't misunderstand: You do need to take a step to follow Jesus and to become a Christian. God, in a miraculous way, delivers you, just as He delivered the people of Israel. The minute you get on the other side, there will be celebration, but this is *not* the Promised Land.

If you understand the geography of Israel, the promised land is not on the banks of the Red Sea. There is the wilderness of Zen, the place of Horab or Sinai, where the law is given, forty years of wandering, and then there is the crossing of the Jordan into the Promised Land. Celebration is always followed by development and maturity. They weren't ready to go into the Promised Land.

During those times when you're struggling with daily life, remember that God is walking with you, carrying you all the way. There will be days of celebration ahead.

Prayer: *Sing to the Lord a new song.*
Sing praises to His name.
Praise the Lord, O my soul.
I thank you, Father, for these people who mean so much to me. (Name them.) Amen.

SOMETIMES I'M UP,
SOMETIMES I'M DOWN

38. Frustration

Exodus 15:22b, 23 *For three days, they traveled in the desert without finding water. When they came to Marah, they could not drink its water because it was bitter.*

How is it that God delivers His people, lets them rejoice in what happens, and then leads them into frustration? The Israelites were on their way to Marah without water. It took three days to get there. After the first day, someone probably said, "It sure would be nice if we had some water." Then on the second day, they said, "We *must* have some water." On the third day, as they came across the crest of the hill and looked down at that enormous pond of water, a beautiful oasis, they probably broke ranks and rushed to begin drinking. Then, one person after another must have said, "This water is bitter. No one told us we were going to have bitter water out here in the desert." And the murmuring against Moses began.

Perhaps you have celebrated what God has done for you, but remember that joy and exultation sometimes are followed by the bitter waters of Marah. For instance, when you got married, it was a glorious, happy experience. There was great celebration, with presents and parties. You walked down the aisle, the words were said, and two became one. Six months, a year, or even twenty years later, you've walked away from the Red Sea — the celebration — and moved to the waters of Marah. The marriage has become bitter, and you want to cut and run. Or it may be that your career was going great, and your dreams of reaching the top were about to come through, when a change of leadership in the corporation shifted you around or even out. High celebration is always followed by the bitter waters of Marah. Life is not always even; it has its ups and downs all the time. Red Sea and celebration . . . Marah and frustration.

Now, what did Moses do? God had already prepared him for this. Remember, Moses had been in the wilderness for forty years before he went back to get the children of Israel. God had gotten him ready, because he was educated in Pharaoh's court, but God had also taught him the ways of the wilderness. The Arabs and Bedouins knew that the way to sweeten brackish water was to put certain filters in it. They cut down a tree that had porous bark, put the tree in the water, and dragged it up and down the stream until the water

54

was clean and the bitterness was gone. It was a primitive way of filtering the water that the Hebrews didn't know about, because they had only made bricks. But Moses knew, because he had lived out there, and God used Moses' experience to take care of the water.

It doesn't take an unusually spiritual person to see how the tree prefigures the tree that Jesus was crucified on. It also shows that God has given us the filter, the cleansing. God has given us the redemptive element in life in the death of Jesus Christ upon the cross. And the bitter water of a marriage that has gone sour, of bad health, of children who have gone astray, of a job that hasn't worked out right, can be made clean and right when you understand that God in Jesus Christ has filtered out the evil of the world. Those who claim Christ as Savior know the strength and are able to survive even in the midst of bitter water. If you don't know Jesus Christ, nothing has cleansed the waters. You have to drink the bitter waters of life. We must drink the water that is here, but the filter, the tree, the cross of Jesus Christ, can make it right.

Prayer: *Dear Father, sometimes the time at the bitter waters of Marah seems very long and tedious. Please teach me to use my experience and knowledge to help bring about the cleansing of this experience. Thank You for providing the redemptive, cleansing filter through Jesus. Let me appreciate more the times of celebration, and keep me open and receptive to more of these opportunities. Amen.*

SOMETIMES I'M UP,
SOMETIMES I'M DOWN

39. Aggravation

Exodus 15:24a *So the people murmured against Moses.*

These were some of the most aggravating people God had ever let live on the face of the earth. Not only did they have antipathy between them, but they also had sheer stubborness. This is not a negative insight into the character of the people; it is an insight into habits and behavior. These were slaves who were not free, and it takes time to make a disciplined people out of freed slaves. They did not have the experience of the desert and they were very unhappy, and they murmured against Moses.

"Murmur" in the Biblical sense is much worse than rumor or gossip; it is very much akin to insurrection. They didn't just murmur; they were ready to kill Moses. (Incidentally, you might be interested to know that the word "murmur" is used infrequently in the Old Testament. There are other words used for rumor, but murmur is used to denote an attitude of insurrection that comes out of the heart of men, as they try to change things because their hearts are wrong.) Had they forgotten that God had been able to overthrow Pharaoh? Had they forgotten the ten plagues, including the Passover plague? Had they forgotten the parting of the Red Sea, just three or four days earlier? Before you murmur against God and wish to leave the people of God, or wish to find some secular god to deliver you from the bitter waters of life, ask yourself if you've forgotten all that God has done.

The tongue can be a very destructive element. "Sticks and stones may break my bones, but names will hurt me none." That's nonsense. The idle tongue can do more damage than any human being can ever imagine. Jesus said we will be held accountable for every idle word. Don't think, because you're somehow lost in a large group, that no one pays attention to you. The Lord God listens to every word, and every word we utter must pass the judgment of our God. Jesus said, "Out of the abundance of the heart, the mouth speaketh." It was evident that the people were basically sick. They wanted to control their leadership. They did not want the leaders to be controlled and owned by the Lord God.

Leadership, both secular and religious, needs to be positive and productive. A leader with a negative, sourpuss attitude will slowly infect all the people with whom he has contact, and the illness will spread like a plague. A pleasant, positive attitude will accomplish more than negative, harsh words every time.

If your life is infected with the disease of murmuring, why don't you ask God's help to change?

Prayer: *Dear Father, some days I am so weary that all my words and actions become negative. Please help me to put a special effort into having a positive attitude. Give me the ability and grace to be an encourager to my family and friends. Amen.*

SOMETIMES I'M UP,
SOMETIMES I'M DOWN

40. Healing

Exodus 15:26,27 *He [God] said, "If you listen carefully to the voice of the Lord your God and do what is right in His eyes, if you pay attention to His commands and keep all His decrees, I will not bring on you any of the diseases I brought on the Egyptians, for I am the Lord who heals you." Then they came to Elim, where there were twelve springs and seventy palm trees, and they camped there near the water.*

God is infinitely loving and patient. How thankful we should be for that! Moses was a little impatient, but who can blame him? He was caught between the murmuring crowd and God. God gave the people a new insight into His nature when He said, "I am the Lord who heals you." God didn't change; they grew up a little bit and learned more about God.

There are days when we're up, and there are days when we're down. We have learned more about God in the shadows of life than in the sunshine. We've learned more about God while weeping in the night than while celebrating in the day.

The people of Israel learned that God is a God who heals people, a God who is in the midst of their bitter waters and experiences. The cross of Christ does that for each one of us, for God is interested in the preservation of His people. God takes them from Marah, from the bitter water, to the oasis of Elim. *El* in a proper name in the Old Testament means "God;" so they went to God's oasis. It is interesting that when they got there, the water was sweet. There were twelve wells, one for each tribe, and seventy palm trees, one for each of the elders of Israel.

Isn't it interesting to see that God leads us out of bondage through the coming of a person in Jesus Christ, born again in a people of God? From celebration to frustration to aggravation, but God is sure that He wants to preserve us. And we would not appreciate the sweet waters of Elim if we had not been through the bitter waters of Marah.

As God deals with your life, He leads and He heals. Never underestimate the fact that God is concerned about healing the human spirit. God leads through the desert and the oasis, and although it is not always celebration, He is always God.

Prayer: *O Lord, thank You for being so loving and patient with me. I seem to have difficulty learning to depend on Your guidance in my life. I also pray for my family and friends. Please touch my grumbling neighbor, my irritable boss, my searching adolescent son. (Name the people you are concerned about.) Allow me to be a blessing in Your name to someone in need of healing today. Amen.*

FRESH EVERY MORNING

41. The Good Old Days

Exodus 16:2,3 *In the desert, the whole community grumbled [murmured] against Moses and Aaron. "If only we had died by the Lord's hand in Egypt! There, we sat around pots of meat and ate all the food we wanted, but you have brought us out into this desert to starve this entire assembly to death."*

While the Israelites were camped at the beautiful oasis of Elim, where water was sweet and food was plentiful, they were pretty well satisfied. We imagine that when Moses went through the camp to tell them it was time to leave to go on to the sacred mountain, there were many who said they were happy there; it was nice and they were content to stay. But God had called His people not to stop at Elim, but to go down to Sinai, where the Law would be given so that they could become a nation. Then they would go on into the Promised Land.

They were six weeks out of bondage and still an infant people. Never let us think that God somehow lets us become instantly full-grown as Christians. That isn't His way. God's way is to move us a step at a time and, as we do this, we come to be the kind of people He wants us to be.

All over camp there was murmuring. They were talking about how bad it was. "Why did we ever listen to Moses? Why did we let him talk us into leaving the wonderful place where we've been?" They had forgotten about the whips across their backs, and that they cried out continually unto God to give them deliverance. All they could think about was that in Egypt, Pharaoh occasionally had given them goat meat to eat, and it was a wonderful existence they were remembering now.

This was before Moses had organized them, and each morning the people would line up outside his tent to complain and murmur. Finally, Moses had enough of this. He realized that they weren't murmuring against him, but they were actually murmuring against God. That's the way it is with us. When we complain about our problems in life, we're really murmuring against the universe.

The children of Isreal complained that they wanted to go back. You know, we grew up thinking that only old people loved the past.

60

Sometimes, in fact, we think of old people as being locked in the past and spending all of their time in restrospect. But it is not necessarily old people who always murmur and want to go back to the old days. Some people have picked a time five or ten years ago that was so good that they just don't want anything to change. There is nothing older, however, than the queen of the prom the day after. Some people who have had great times in high school can't quite get away from that experience. Yesterday's All-American is still walking around telling how it used to be. There is nothing worse than people living in the past. God didn't call us to stay in the past.

People who are living in the present have been down the road and know what it is to be marred and scarred and buffeted by life. They are accustomed to carrying the load of life, and they know you won't stay at the bitter waters and you can't stay at the oasis. You have to go on; life calls you on. You're going to get hurt. Life has a way of putting some scars on you. You may see it all wash away, but that doesn't mean life is over. All it means is that God is working with you and leading you. You can stop and grumble all you want to, but life goes on. When you've been scarred, when you've bled, when you've cried, then you're able to look at life and understand that you don't have to pretend. You don't have to hold happiness in, for fear that something is going to get it. You find out that the important things survive. God is with you.

Prayer: *Father, I thank You for this day. It matters not whether it is rainy or sunny; I am just thankful for the opportunities the day may bring. Make me sensitive to the needs of others. Give me grace to cope with whatever life brings today. Amen.*

61

FRESH EVERY MORNING

42. Gather His Manna Daily

Exodus 16:11 *The Lord said to Moses, "I have heard the grumbling of the Israelites. Tell them, 'At twilight you will eat meat, and in the morning you will be filled with bread. Then you will know that I am the Lord your God.'"*

Bread from heaven, or manna, as the Israelites named it, is one of the marvels of the Bible. God gave specific instructions on the gathering of this wafer-like substance. It had to be gathered early in the morning or it would melt away with the heat of the sun. They were to gather only enough for the day's needs; the leftovers would attract maggots and stink. He was teaching His people to depend on Him for their needs. They were dependent on Him not only for nourishment, but also for spiritual bread.

God provides spiritual manna for all of us. You can't gather it up for the future; it will spoil. God gives enough strength to sustain us throughout our times of trouble and turmoil. The problem with most of us is that we don't gather the manna. We want to be spoon-fed, or at least have someone go out and gather it for us. It isn't fun to get up early every morning to gather spiritual manna.

This also involves trust. We can gather only a daily amount, so we have to believe that God will not forget to provide for tomorrow. He will not fail to provide. Will you fail to gather daily?

Prayer: *Dear God, why do I become so anxious and fearful? I know that You will provide spiritual strength for me, if only I will avail myself of it. Thank You for providing for me at all times, and especially in times of deep distress. Amen.*

FRESH EVERY MORNING

43. Never on Sunday

Exodus 16:29a, 30 *"Bear in mind that the Lord has given you the Sabbath; that is why on the sixth day He gives you bread for two days." . . . So the people rested on the seventh day.*

All busy people yearn for a day of rest. God Himself gave His permission, a command even, for a day to allow the soul and spirit to be refreshed. This is really God's gift to us. He will take care of us physically and spiritually if we follow His plan. Our systems need a time of replenishment. Sunday is a special day for this worship and refreshment.

During the gold rush days, two wagon trains were headed west. Their destination was the gold fields of California. The first wagon train decided to push hard and get there first, so they traveled seven days a week. The second wagon train decided to take one day a week to rest the horses and themselves, and to have church and praise God. Well, the first wagon train charged ahead and arrived in Mississippi before the other train. They were excited. They pushed harder. After a number of weeks of this pressure, however, the people began arguing among themselves. Then the wagons started breaking down, and the horses had problems. Everything and everybody broke down. Needless to say, the second wagon train arrived at the gold fields long before the first one. The train that took a Sabbath to worship and rest withstood the rigors of that difficult journey much better. They were people with souls made to worship God.

What about you? Have you allowed yourself the joy of a Sabbath? Have you enjoyed the revitalizing experience of worship?

Prayer: *The Lord is my shepherd, I shall lack nothing. He makes me lie down in green pastures; He leads me beside quiet waters; He restores my soul. He guides me in paths of righteousness for His name's sake. Psalm 23: 1,2,3*

FRESH EVERY MORNING

44. For Generations to Come

Exodus 16:32 *Moses said, "This is what the Lord has commanded: 'Take an omer of manna and keep it for the generations to come, so they can see the bread I gave you to eat in the desert when I brought you out of Egypt.'"*

The people were murmuring again. They really didn't want to pay the price for freedom. The rigors of desert life had softened the harshness of slavery in their memories. Aren't people funny? Life under Pharaoh's whip was pure misery, but when instant freedom didn't materialize, they grumbled. God wanted to make sure that in the years to come, the children would be told of and the people would always remember the constant care and nurture of God. They wanted to go back to the past. God, in His wisdom, told Moses to take an omer of manna, put it in a jar, and keep it with the holy things of Israel, so that it would become part of their worship experience.

Look at your life. Are you mumbling and grumbling? Do you think life has been harsh on you? Have you remembered that God feeds you everyday, and that all you have to do is gather it?

Perhaps it is time to stop and look at the manna you are preserving. You need to understand that in the dark places of your existence, God has been with you. He has delivered you, brought you out of bondage, and nourished you, and He will continue to carry you on.

One of the best ways to preserve a measure of manna today is to keep a notebook, a prayer diary. Write down at least one gift from God each day. As you look back, remembering in years to come, you'll be amazed at the goodness and grace of God. His gifts are fresh every day.

Prayer: *Father, forgive my grumbling words, my negative attitude. Thank You for the day you have given me, and help me to be a blessing to someone. Amen. (Write down some blessings of today.)*

A TREASURED POSSESSION

45. On Eagles' Wings

Exodus 19:3, 6a . . . *and the Lord called to him [Moses] from the mountain and said, "This is what you are to say to the house of Jacob and what you are to tell the people of Israel: 'You yourselves have seen what I did to Egypt, and how I carried you on eagles' wings and brought you to myself.'"*

God chose a very powerful image to describe to His people how they had been carried through very troubled times. The eagle has symbolized power and majesty, strength and courage, since ancient times. The Israelites were familiar with the eagle. They had watched these magnificent birds, as they soared high in the sky. It was not unusual to see the parent eagles urging their young to fly off on their own. If the young eagle faltered, the parent would swoop under the baby and carry it to safety on powerful wings.

Through the years, the eagle has been used to symbolize renewed vigor. "My youth is renewed like the eagle's" (Psalm 103:5b). Now God is reminding His people that they really are His: ". . . and brought you to myself." He is saying that through all those difficulties, the rigors of slavery, the terrors of escape, He was with them in a powerful way.

Is God reminding you that He has carried you through many dangers, storms, and stresses, and brought you to Him?

The eagle is also the symbol of generosity. It was believed that the eagle, no matter how great its hunger, always left half its prey to the birds that followed. We don't have to be reminded that God is generous and desires that quality in His children, also.

With faith in God, we can be carried as on eagles' wings through whatever life brings. We are His treasured possession.

Prayer: *Father, when I am worn, and weary of soul and body, let me remember the encouraging words of the prophet Isaiah: "Don't you understand? Don't you know by now that the everlasting God, the Creator of the farthest parts of the earth, never grows faint or weary? No one can fathom the depths of His understanding. He gives power to the tired and worn-out, and strength to the weak. Even the youths shall* be exhausted, and the young men will all give up. But they that wait upon the Lord shall renew their strength; they shall mount up with wings like eagles; they shall run and not be weary; they shall walk and not faint." (Isaiah 40:28,31) I claim that promise today, O Lord. Amen.

A TREASURED POSSESSION

46. Obey My Voice

Exodus 19:5 *"Now, if you obey me fully and keep my covenant, then out of all nations you will be my treasured possession."*

If there is a deadness in your spiritual life, it may be that the answer is in this verse. Our relationship to God is a covenant, a contract. Too often we forget that we have a part to uphold, and we expect God to continually "cover" for us.

"Obey" is such an archaic word, and we desire complete independence so desperately that to "obey God's voice" is an offense to our psyche. We expect God to work wonders with a life that has broken every law of the universe.

Not long ago, a child was playing with a group of children in a park. They were supervised by mothers and babysitters. Suddenly, one little girl broke from the group and ran as fast as lightning toward a busy street. Her mother, and all the other mothers, shouted and screamed for her to stop. The child glanced over her shoulder several times, so they knew she heard, but she ran out of the park and in front of a truck too quickly for the driver to swerve. The child survived but is crippled for life.

Could that be a picture of how it is with your life? Are you running as fast as you can, hearing the voice of God, but saying under your breath, "Not yet. I can't stop now?" The next question comes when you're hurt and bruised almost beyond repair. We hear it all the time: "Why me, Lord?" Think of how different life might be if we could only learn to say, "Teach me, Lord, and I will hear."

Prayer: *How could areas of your life change if you began to listen and obey God? Write them down. Now pray about them. Ask God to give you the ability and the desire to obey. Amen.*

A TREASURED POSSESSION

47. Keep My Covenant

Deuteronomy 7:7, 8a, 9b *The Lord did not set his affection on you and choose you because you were more numerous than other people, for you were the fewest of all people. But it was because the Lord loved you and kept the oath He swore to your forefathers that He brought you out with a mighty hand and redeemed you from the land of slavery . . . He is the faithful God, keeping His covenant of love to a thousand generations of those who love Him and keep His commands.*

This scripture in Deuteronomy goes on to expand the covenant relationship that is emphasized in Exodus. God made a contract with His people, and obedience was the necessary ingredient on their part. These were conditional promises made to these people, whom He chose above all others to love in a very special way.

We are quick to judge those newly freed slaves for their inability to be faithful. Trust is a vital ingredient in a covenant relationship. The Israelites failed to be able to trust God completely for all their needs. They never understood the depth of His love.

Are we much better than they? He is the faithful God, and we are blessed with the treasure of reassurances in the Bible. It all boils down to this: "Can I really trust God to take care of my life, to love me, and keep His word?"

It is difficult to trust anyone these days, especially if you don't know the person very well. People hurt each other terribly, and, for the sake of safety, we doubt everybody. You can trust one who loves you and has your best interest at heart.

Prayer: *Ask God to increase your level of trust. Write down two recent events that show that God loves you. Add this to your prayer: "I trust in You, Lord, and want to do good; I commit my way to You; I trust in Your unfailing love, and I will praise You forever for what You have done. In Your name, I have hope." Amen.*

A TREASURED POSSESSION

48. A Call to Minister

Exodus 19:5b, 6a. *"Although the whole earth is mine, you will be for me a kingdom of priests and a holy nation."*

A whole nation of priests should produce a wonderful environment in which to live. Israel had a very special relationship to God, and, because of this, God called its people into ministry. Israel was the forerunner of the church, and this is a commandment to the church. We are to relate in a ministering way to our extended family, the church.

To be God's holy nation was a wondrous honor. The word "holy" is defined as "being specially recognized or declared sacred." These were a sacred people, whom God loved above all the other people on earth.

You are a specially recognized person. You are God's sacred, holy creation, whom He loves dearly. He made the ultimate sacrifice, His only son (John 3:16), so that you may have eternal life with Him. You may not be feeling very special and certainly not very holy or sacred, but you are. You are God's chosen.

Prayer: *O Lord, You have searched me and You know me. You know when I sit and when I rest; You perceive my thoughts from afar. You discern my going out and my lying down; You are familiar with all my ways. Before a word is on my tongue, You know it completely, O Lord. You hem me in, behind and before; You have laid Your hand upon me. Such knowledge is too wonderful for me, too lofty for me to attain. I praise You because I am fearfully and wonderfully made; Your works are wonderful, I know that full well. Psalm 139:1-6,14. Amen.*

A TREASURED POSSESSION

49. A Call to Consecration

Exodus 19:10, 11, 12a. *And the Lord said to Moses, "Go to the people and consecrate them today and tomorrow. Have them wash their clothes and be ready by the third day, because on that day, the Lord will come down on Mount Sinai in the sight of all the people. Put limits for the people around the mountain."*

Do you ever feel that life is so busy that there isn't room for one more thing? There are days when getting children to and from school, scouts and music lessons, running errands, shopping for the best bargains, and preparing meals, leaves one wondering if there is any part of life that is holy. Some days are filled with letters to write, an important campaign to present, a product to sell, a business to keep afloat, people to mollify. There is no time to consider the holy areas of life.

Perhaps we need to read this message to the Israelites from God with present day meanings. Consecration can be interpreted as "sacred, holy," or separated from the world of common things. In the Biblical sense, holiness or consecration is really a matter of dedication to God. It is a positive action, not merely a withdrawal from unholy living.

We desire spirit-filled lives while determined to consume, absorb, and participate in the whole smorgasbord of our culture. Someone said that we are not required by God to *do* something obedient, but to *be* someone obedient. Spiritual vitality comes when we learn to set limits, to cut out the excesses, so that we can be prepared for what God has ready for us next. Neutrality is not acceptable. We really have only two possibilities — to obey God or to disobey God with our lives. God told Moses to set the limits for the people. God set limits for you, for all of us, too.

Prayer: *Dear Father, teach me the limits for my life, so that I can experience Your spirit in my life. Let me be obedient, let me consecrate my life to be what You want me to be. Let the peripheral things be dropped, and open my vision to Your leadership. Amen.*

A TREASURED POSSESSION

50. The Coming of the Lord

Exodus 19:16, 17 *On the morning of the third day, there was thunder and lightning, with a thick cloud over the mountain, and a very loud trumpet blast. Everyone in the camp trembled. Then Moses led the people out of the camp to meet with God, and they stood at the foot of the mountain. Mount Sinai was covered with smoke, because the Lord descended on it in fire.*

The people were finally ready for Moses to lead them out of the camp to meet God. How would you describe the coming of the Lord? What an exciting, frightening experience! God had to make certain that His chosen people understood His nature. He was not to be mistaken for one of the many gods of the other nations. God must teach His chosen ones that the Lord our God is one God, and we must worship Him in spirit and in truth. So God carefully showed the people His power and might.

Can you just imagine the feelings of the people as they waited at the foot of the mountain? They were willing to make a covenant with God, in order to receive His blessings. They consecrated themselves, acknowledged the limits set for them by God through Moses. The third day dawned with thunder, lightning, a trumpet blast, and smoke on the mountain. Then God spoke through the thunder, and Moses interpreted God's message.

This is a statement dealing with the Lord's call to covenant life; it shows God's challenge to man to become the unique possession of the Lord. This is relevant today. The people of Israel had Moses as their mediator. He led them to meet the Lord. Today we have Jesus, who is our mediator, our comfort, and guide. God breaks into our lives, confronts us and challenges us to live the covenant life. When we consecrate ourselves according to the Lord's directions, He breaks through and discloses His will through personal encounter.

Have you heard the trumpet blast and the thunder roll? Have you seen the lightning and the smoke on the mountain? God is trying to break through and claim you for His precious possession.

Prayer: *Father, it is very hard to be committed to the covenant life today. I don't even understand what You want, except that You want me. Give me the ability to trust my life to Your hands and to be able to pray with sincerity, "Thy will be done." Amen.*

REQUIREMENTS FOR COMMITMENT

51. Principles of Character

Exodus 19:1, 2b *In the third month after the Israelites left Egypt – on the very day – they came to the desert of Sinai. . . . and Israel camped there in the desert in front of the mountain.*

Moses had safely delivered the people of Israel to the foot of Mount Sinai, and God assured Moses that this was, indeed, His will. He spoke to Moses and gave instructions for the receiving of the laws the people were to live by. After the Hebrews received the law, they would be personally responsible to God for their actions. The laws were given so that the people would have principles on which to base their lives, so that they could have a relationship with God. God is always more interested in a relationship with His people than He is in laws. The laws were to make it possible for the people to be God's peculiar, precious possession.

Several years ago, while visiting the city of Seoul, Korea, we were impressed with the fact that trees had been planted all over by the government. These small saplings were terribly vulnerable to the elements. Seoul is very crowded, and the people moving across the city sometimes had been prone to push the trees over. The government, in order to protect the trees, had built small braces around them. These braces were very strong and rugged. They were there for the express purpose of making sure that the trees were not trampled or pulled up.

That's exactly what God did when He brought the fledgling nation out of bondage. These people were not ready to go into the Promised Land. They had had four hundred and thirty years in bondage, with the Egyptians telling them what to do. They had come through the bitter experiences of the waters of Marah, to the sweet waters of Elim, and had learned to eat manna in the wilderness. Now they had come to the foot of Mount Sinai, where God would put the brace around them. God was going to make them into a nation, and a nation is not brought into being overnight. When a person is converted, he doesn't become an instant, strong, mature Christian; he is a babe and has to grow. God understands this, and places a brace around us so that we can grow as we should.

We have these ten commandments, which are not suggestions for being religious, but rather principles that God has given for the strengthening of life and the Christian experience. It takes courage to come out of bondage and cross the Red Sea. It takes courage to be the person God has called you to be. But it takes more than courage to be a nation. It takes character. The courage had already been given to them in the leadership of Moses as they came out of bondage, and once they were ready to become a nation, character was needed.

Freedom can become a very dangerous thing, if you don't have the character to go with it. Some people have lost freedom in the name of freedom. For instance, a man could say he's free to drink, but in being free to drink, he becomes an alcoholic. Young people say they are free to use drugs, but in that freedom, they become addicts. Other people have said that they are free to experiment with extramarital sex, only to find that their marriage disintegrates. You cannot have any kind of freedom until you have a brace built around it to give strength. God understood this, so He gave us the law, and then as the nation grew and roots went deeper, a new revelation came in Jesus Christ.

Prayer: *Father, thank You for setting up the fences for my life. Let me not try to destroy them, or I will destroy myself. Thank You for the freedom to live inside the limits You set. I thank You for caring enough to make me Your precious treasure. Amen.*

REQUIREMENTS FOR COMMITMENT

52. I Am the Lord

Exodus 20:2 *"I am the Lord your God, who brought you out of Egypt out of the land of slavery."*

Covenants in the ancient Near East always began with a preamble stating the author. It is interesting to note that the Lord alone was mentioned. It is not a joint covenant between Israel and the Lord; it is a covenant originating in the sovereignty of God over man. The preamble describes God's gracious and redemptive act of deliverance and identifies the speaker as the one God, the deliverer of Israel, who has the right to command absolute obedience.

Sometimes we tend to think that God was harsh with His people, when He so plainly gave them (and us) rules for living. Actually He is gracious in instructing us in the best way to live. God always acts redemptively with His most precious creation. "I am the Lord your God, who brought you out of . . . slavery." Are you still in bondage? Remember how you "peeled the hide" off your spouse with those words of anger? Have you assumed the role of judge, jury, and executioner toward all people? Are the chains of anger making you powerless? Is a sour attitude strangling you? If the Lord brought the Hebrews out of slavery, with all of their problems to overcome, He is capable of setting you free.

Prayer: *Many, O Lord my God, are the wonders you have done. The things you have planned for us no one can recount to you; were I to speak and tell of them, they would be too many to declare.*

Sacrifice and offering you did not desire, but my ears you have pierced, burnt offerings and sin offerings you did not require.

Then I said, "Here I am, I have come – it is written about me in the scroll. To do your will, O my God, is my desire; your law is written within my heart." Psalm 40:5-8

REQUIREMENTS FOR COMMITMENT

53. Who Do You Worship? (Commandment I)

Exodus 20:3 *"You shall have no other gods before me."*

The Bible does not present arguments for the existence of God. It is overwhelmingly emphatic about who God is. It begins with the words, "In the beginning, God . . ." The first commandment begins by establishing the fact that this God will be the supreme God for our lives. The Bible doesn't say, "Let's sit down and decide whether or not there is a God." It begins by saying that God shall be your God, and He will have priority and be supreme in your life.

The commandments fall into two categories. The first four have to do with God's relationship to man; the last six have to do with man's relationship to man. A college professor asked a group of students to take the ten commandments and arrange them as they would best fit their lives. Every student put the man-to-man ones at the top, and the ones having to do with our relationship to God at the bottom.

Now, God is wiser than man, and He knows that we have to get our relationship to Him right before we can have our relationships with one another right. The commandments come together in such a way that God is supreme, and that our relationship to God is the thing that we must get in the proper place; everything else comes from it. These commandments, as they place God first, establish which god man will worship.

The Hebrews had come out of bondage from a nation where there were all kinds of gods. There was a god of the sun and a god of the harvest, a god of fertility and a god of the Nile. There was a god for everything. They had a very cloudy definition in their own mind of the God of Abraham, Isaac, and Jacob, for they were seeing Him for the first time. Some of them probably had little golden images in their baggage as they came out, so that when they doubted the existence of the God who had parted the Red Sea, they would have these gods to bow down to. But God makes it clear — no false gods.

We live in a world that is filled with gods. Modern man has become so sophisticated that he has rearranged them. He has not deified them in the same way they did in ancient times, by building shrines to them, but modern man has his gods.

76

Prayer: *Name some of your gods. Perhaps you will have some of these: money, prestige, family, education, indifference. What does it mean to have a God? Martin Luther said that a person's God is whatever his heart clings to and relies on.*

O, Father, teach me Your ways, for You are my only God, my Savior. My heart clings to You . . . hold me close. Amen.

REQUIREMENTS FOR COMMITMENT

54. No Other Gods (Commandment I)

Exodus 20:3 *"You shall have no other gods before me."*

Modern man worships many gods. The Lord God who gave this commandment has many rivals for our total commitment. The first god that tries to rival the Lord God of the ages is the god of individualism. Individualism is nothing but selfishness deified. It is pride put on the throne. Individualism, the worship of what is right for you alone, is pure selfishness and ego. We see people who walk away from any commitment if it doesn't satisfy all their "needs." You've heard someone say, "My marriage doesn't fulfill me, therefore I'm leaving."

There is also another god on the throne in America. That's the god of materialism. He's an ancient god, and we've worshipped him along with the Lord God for a long time. Every generation has to find out that the god of materialism doesn't satisfy. We believe that the world God made is good. He said of His creation, "It is good." However, we take His creation and use it the wrong way. Some have sold their souls to gather things — materialism. The worship of things has left us as a generation of empty people.

In our modern society, we also have come to believe that big business and technology are holy. We forget that the God who made us will not share the stage with another god. Business can fail overnight, technology can blow a fuse, but the Lord God is ever-present, demanding our first allegiance.

The first commandment is really a call to get priorities right. If your life is just limping along, if there is no hum or harmony in your life, it may be that your priorities are mixed up. Remember that He commands, "You shall have no other gods before me."

Prayer: *Lord, let me learn that religion cannot be just a preference, but must be a passion for me. Jesus said, "Love the Lord your God with all your heart and with all your soul and with all your mind. This is the first and greatest commandment." (Matthew 22:37,38) Help me to get my priorities in order, that I may live according to this commitment. Amen.*

REQUIREMENTS FOR COMMITMENT

55. How Do You Worship? (Commandment II)

Exodus 20:4, 5a *"You shall not make for yourself an idol in the form of anything in heaven above or on the earth beneath or in the waters below. You shall not bow down to them or worship them . . ."*

If there has ever been a time when we needed to examine the words of God, it is today. We have lost our compass bearing; we don't know what's right any more. We no longer follow the North Star of morality. For six decades, we have sown the seeds of materialism and humanism. We have gone into uninhibited sex; drugs, liquor, and pornography abound in our culture. We live in a day that is filled with moral anarchy, which causes our nation to fall into ruin. What are we going to do about this? Should we wring our hands and walk off to the side and say, "Woe is me?" Or do we cry with the prophet of old, "Cry aloud, spare not, lift up thy voice like the trumpet, show the people their transgression?"

People are not sure what is right and wrong any more. It's time for good men to cry out, to lift up their voices like trumpets, and to say something about the moral wickedness in which we find ourselves. Some of us feel like Dylan Thomas. We're caught in a situation where we're too proud to cry and too frail to check the tears; we're caught between two nights — blindness and death.

God gave this commandment to Moses, who gave it to the people. They had just come out of Egypt where they had observed the pagans worshipping gods with heads like falcons and bodies like men. When the Israelites came out of Egypt, they may have stolen one or two of the little golden idols to have just in case the God of Moses didn't work things out. First God says to the people, "You shall have no other gods before me." Then He tells them not to make an idol or graven image. Is God repeating Himself?

The first commandment tells us who we should worship; the second commandment tells us how. The first commandment tells us that we should worship Jehovah exclusively; the second commandment says we should worship Him spiritually. The first commandment talks about the unity of God; the second commandment talks about the spirituality of God.

Sometimes people feel the need to use some kind of crutch to remind them of God — a picture, a symbol, or a cloth. After a while,

79

the use of the crutch can become in itself the worship of a thing. There is an easy transition from being reminded by a thing to worshipping that thing. The God of the universe, the invisible God who spoke to Moses through the burning bush and told him to call the people out of bondage, will not be reduced to a graven image.

A little boy was talking to his mother while she was busy doing something else, and he couldn't get her attention. He kept pulling at her and asking, "Mother, is God everywhere?" Most mothers aren't willing to get caught up in a theological discussion with a five-year-old child over the presence of God. "Yes, son, God is everywhere," she answered. The child continued, "If God is everywhere, is he in this room?" The answer was yes. "Well, if God is everywhere, and if he is in this room, is he in this little jar I have?" Now, you can't argue with that kind of logic, so again the answer was yes. With that, the little boy put the cap on the jar and said, "I've got you now, God; you can't get away!"

When we make idols, we do the same thing to God — we bottle Him up. He can't be any more than that. Any time you use a word to describe God, you limit Him. God is bigger than language. God is righteous; He's more than righteous. If God is love, He is more than love. We can't find a word, an idol, an institution, or a creed that describes God or contains Him, and that's what this commandment is saying.

Prayer: *Father, we are exposed to so many forms of immorality every day. It is easy to become calloused and just accept it. Let worship become an integral part of my life. "Yet a time is coming, and has now come when the true worshiper will worship the Father in spirit and truth, for they are the kind of worshipers the Father seeks. God is spirit, and His worshipers must worship in spirit and truth." (John 4:23, 24) Amen.*

REQUIREMENTS FOR COMMITMENT

56. Tough Love (Commandment II)

Exodus 20:5b, 6 *". . . for I the Lord your God, am a jealous God, punishing the children for the sin of the fathers to the third and fourth generation of those who hate me, but showing love to thousands who love me and keep my commandments."*

God was saying something to His people about love. Jealousy is one of the consequences of love. The relationship between God and Israel is frequently spoken of in the Old Testament as that between husband and wife. God loves Israel as His wife whom He rescued from an aggressor, and when she is unfaithful to Him, He is angry, for He is jealous. When the word *jealous* is used to describe God's feelings, it is not the same as human jealousy. Human jealousy is often unfounded and suspicious and mean. Divine jealousy is a measure of God's love for His people. He was jealous of Israel, and this is carried over to the church as the bride of Christ. Jesus demands love that takes precedence over any natural relationship.

God will not tolerate any rival claims on the lives of His people. He will not tolerate the idols stuck back in the corners of your life. God is not indifferent; He cares enough to react, to respond.

When a child has openly disobeyed and seemingly is determined to defy parental authority, he must be punished to assure him that his parents love and care enough to punish him.

This passionate, intense love of God for man is ultimately revealed in Jesus Christ. This jealous love is also the love expressed in John 3:16 . . . "For God so loved the world that He gave His only son . . . that we might have eternal life." And this is the blessing we inherit — eternal life.

Prayer: *Father, burn this commandment into my heart and mind. Forgive me when I am unfaithful to You. Let me put aside all the things that stand in the way of my relationship with You. Thank You for loving so much and caring so deeply for me. Amen.*

REQUIREMENTS FOR COMMITMENT

57. Under Whose Name? (Commandment III)

Exodus 20:7 *You shall not misuse the name of the Lord your God, for the Lord will not hold anyone guiltless who misuses his name.*

Do you remember the wonderful stories about Winnie the Pooh by Milne? Our family grew up loving and identifying with Eeyore, the donkey who whines and complains; Kanga, constant mother; Roo, the eternal child; Rabbit, the gadabout; and Pooh, the happy, bumbling, overweight bear, who loves Christopher Robin, the father figure of them all. Pooh had no last name, but he lived under the name of "Sanders" in the forest. Actually, there was a sign on a tree that said "Sanders," and Pooh lived under that sign.

That's a long story to get to a very small point, but some of you are living under names a lot less significant. Everybody lives under some name; a lot of people, it seems, are living under the names of New York designers. In the clothing business years ago, we always said that if we could ever find a way to get the label on the outside of the suit, we would double our sales volume. Now, it's finally happened. Everyone lives under some name. You may go under the name of your family, or you may go under the name of your God, or you may go under the name of your false gods, but everybody goes under a name.

The third commandment is one that we overlook many times, because we don't understand the power and impact of the concept of names in the ancient Near East, and particularly with the Hebrews. God said there is one God, and we are not to worship Him in idols. Then He said for us to work and live under His name. The impact was great because the idea of name in the Old Testament is one of the strongest concepts ever known among men. In the ancient Near East, the name was literally the person. They were not to live under idols or pagan gods; they were to live under the name of the invisible God that met Moses in the wilderness. The name of that God was the person of that God. The name became not a symbol for the person, but the person himself.

In the twentieth-century mind, a name is the symbol of a person and calls to mind that person. But in the Biblical concept, the name of the person written down *is* that person. To insult you simply required insulting your name. To honor you required honoring your name. The literal writing of it was the person. For instance, Jacob, when he stole the birthright from Esau, was called the "supplanter, one who takes the place of another." Later he had a great religious experience in his struggle with God, and his name was changed to Israel, "one who strives with God."

The names were important. The names of the books in the Old and New Testament have meanings, too. Isaiah means "salvation;" Malachi, the last book of the Old Testament, means "the Lord's messenger, or the angel of the Lord who comes to speak the message." The name Jeremiah means "that the Lord hurls him forward." Jesus means "salvation." The person was actually present in the name. It's interesting that when we worship, we are told to "call" upon the name of the Lord. You recall that when Moses was struggling with God before the burning bush, he said, "Who are You, what is Your name? When I go before Pharaoh and all those people in bondage, they're going to ask me what the name of my God is, and I need to know Your name." God said, "Tell them that I Am sent you."

Israel had no idols, but Israel had the name, the essence, and the presence of God. So, when we talk about "hallowed be thy name" in the New Testament in the prayer that Jesus gave us, we talk about making the actual name of God holy with our lives. The commandment says not to take the name of God in vain. Most people have construed that to mean not to cuss, and particularly not to use a profane expression that says something negative about God.

Let's look at the word "vain." It's used fifty-three times in the Old Testament. In the Old Testament sense, the writer is saying "emptiness." It's the picture of a balloon with nothing but air in it; a picture of something that is hollow, unfulfilled, and has no purpose. So what God said to Moses was that he should tell the people that, in their worship, they are to have one God, that they are not to worship him in an idol, and that they are not to take His name with emptiness or shallowness.

Prayer: *Heavenly Father, let Your name be holy in my life. I live under Your name, Blessed Savior. I ask Your name, Blessed Savior. I ask Your help to never bring embarrassment to Your name. Amen.*

REQUIREMENTS FOR COMMITMENT

58. Cut-Flower Culture (Commandment III)

Matthew 5:37 *Simply let your "Yes" be "Yes," and your "No, No;" anything beyond this comes from the evil one.*
James 3:9 *With the tongue we praise our Lord and Father, and with it we curse men, who have been made in God's likeness.*

The language we use is a reflection of our inner being. A profane (empty, shallow) person is easy to identify once he opens his mouth. Interestingly enough, profane people usually talk a great deal more than people who try to use care and maturity in conversation. This third commandment has great implication for our speech. The old saying, "One picture is worth a thousand words, so speech doesn't really mean anything," is a lot of nonsense. Language is very important.

Those who work in the State Department say that a diplomat has to speak with precision. Those of you who work in legal firms know that precision of language is important in a document or contract. Let's face it, pictures are beautiful, but a picture can never give you the real sense of the Ten Commandments, the twenty-third Psalm, the Beatitudes, or any of the great parables of Jesus. You can't wrap them up in a thousand words. Language is a living thing among us; it moves, and that's what the Bible understands. There is an objectivity about language; the Old Testament talks about speaking the truth. The New Testament talks about being and doing the truth.

You ask, "What is profanity?" The word "profane" means language that was to be spoken outside the temple. The temple area had its own language, and there were certain words that were not uttered inside the temple area. Those were the profane words.

When our two sons were just little guys, they learned some words that were not normally spoken around our house. One night at the table, one of the boys innocently said one of these words. You can imagine what happened: Chills and fever went all over the table, and we said, "Wait a minute; we don't talk like that." They wanted to know why not, was it just because they were a preacher's kids? We answered that it was just because we don't use profane words, and we decided to find out what makes a word profane.

We did a personal language analysis, and we concluded that a word is profane when it attacks the inner person — when it talks about his heritage, or consigns his soul to hell, or compares him with the worst thing you can think of. These are the things that make a word profane. You can take that definition to another level: We take the Lord's name in vain when we use words in an empty way to hurt people. Gossip is an example of this.

We also break this commandment when we question the motives of someone. "I know what he did, but I wonder what his real motives were." That's the most destructive thing you can do to someone. Only that person and God know the motive. That's a secret place, and when we begin walking around inside someone's life with golf shoes on, questioning their motives, we're on holy ground.

Another way we break this commandment is through the emptiness of our lives. Theologian Elton Trueblood said that our society and our current religion is like a cut-flower society. We all know that flowers do not last very long when they have been cut off from their roots. There is no sustenance coming up into them. They're going to bloom, be cut, arranged, admired, and die. That's a parable of our day. Many people think that if they look good and stand in the right places, wear the right clothes, have the proper approach to everything, but do away with the root that made them what they are, they will be O.K. But the Bible says that is an empty, vain life. It's that kind of commitment that will bring you to destruction.

What are you? A cut flower that will soon wither and be thrown out? Or are you planted firmly, with your roots well watered?

Prayer: *Father, help me to bear a wholesome witness to Your name. Let me not be spiritually illiterate. "May the words of my mouth and the meditation of my heart be pleasing in Your sight, O Lord, my Rock and my Redeemer." (Psalm 19:14) Amen.*

REQUIREMENTS FOR COMMITMENT

59. Remember The Sabbath (Commandment IV)

Exodus 20:7,8,9,11 *"Remember the Sabbath day by keeping it holy. Six days you shall labor and do all your work, but the seventh day is a Sabbath to the Lord your God." . . . For in six days the Lord made the heavens and the earth, the sea, and all that is in them, but He rested on the seventh day. Therefore the Lord blessed the Sabbath day and made it holy.*

Cecil Meyers, pastor of Peachtree Road Methodist Church in Atlanta, tells a story about an expedition going into the heart of the deepest jungles of Africa. The men were anxious to get to a place that reportedly had great treasure. The expedition looked like a scene out of a Tarzan movie, with the great white hunters up front and the African men carrying the burdens behind. Finally, after they had pressed on and on, day after day, the laborers refused to carry the burdens. When asked why, the response was, "You've pressed too hard, and they say now that they want to rest and let their souls catch up with their bodies." That's a parable for us in our day. Somehow, along the way, we have confused God's gift of the Sabbath with all kinds of rules and regulations. The Bible says that it took God six days to create the world, and then He rested. God created us like Himself, and, after a period of work and stress, we need to have a time of rekindling our inner selves. So God gave us the Sabbath.

God never intended for the Sabbath day to be a burden. You may recall the incident in the life of Jesus when He was caught in a Sabbath controversy. He was so disgusted with the way the Sabbath had been weighted with rules and regulations, that He said, "Man was not created for the Sabbath; the Sabbath was created for man." God created us as a holy people, and then He gave a holy day. This holy day is significant. It was a day of rejoicing, a gift of God, a day of no work. The word "Sabbath" does not mean seven; it means cessation, the quitting of work.

Today, in the Arab section of Jerusalem, there is business and commerce on the Sabbath, but in the Jewish section, almost everything is boarded up. There are times when you're not allowed to go through these sections, because it's a violation of the Sabbath. There is strong feeling against anyone who would desecrate it.

The early Christians were obsessed with the fact that they came out of a Jewish background. Yet God did something new and real for them in the Easter experience, so they would have the Sabbath, and so they would gather together as the Christian sect on Sunday morning and celebrate the resurrection.

But there is a difference between the Sabbath and Sunday. You work until the Sabbath, and then you rest. Sunday is the day that gives you strength to work the six days in front of you. The Sabbath is the end of the week; Sunday is the beginning. The Sabbath is from sundown to sundown, but Sunday is from midnight to midnight. The Sabbath is a day of rest, but Sunday is a day of worship. The Sabbath has a penalty to it, if you break it; Sunday has no penalty, except that you shortchange yourself.

The Christian draws his strength from Sunday. It's a time to let God talk to the inner man. It's a time when we make real that practice which says, in effect, "Be still and know that I am God." The Christians took the value of the Hebrew Sabbath and added to it the great joy of the Christian resurrection. We have a marriage of the two in the Christian community.

The commandment said, "Remember the Sabbath Day." So we come together as a body of Christ and remember what God has done. It's a sacrament. Worship and Bible study make Sunday a day when the soul is rekindled, as well as a day when the body is rested. You may miss a dinner party or a trip to the beach by observing the Sabbath, but you won't miss heaven. Your life won't disintegrate. It just depends on how you want to spend your time. You'll have thousands of Sundays in your adult life; how will you spend them?

Prayer: *"This is the day the Lord has made; let us rejoice and be glad in it. You are my God and I will give You thanks; You are my God and I will exalt You. Give thanks to the Lord, for He is good; His love endures forever." (Psalm 118:24,28,29) Amen.*

REQUIREMENTS FOR COMMITMENT

60. Holy Day or Holiday? (Commandment IV)

Exodus 31:12,13 *Then the Lord said to Moses, "Say to the Israelites, 'You must observe my Sabbaths. This will be a sign between me and you for the generations to come, so you may know that I am the Lord, who makes you holy.'"*

Society has gotten caught up in a seven-day, twenty-four-hour-a-day week. Some of you work in a business where you have no control over what you do on Sunday. Some of you are managers of businesses with policies set by someone else in a distant city, and you're caught. You can't get out of it, and you don't know what to do; but you know it's wrong and it violates everything you are.

Thoreau said if you want to destroy the Christian faith, first take away Sunday. He was right; it's a holy day. For those who know Jesus Christ as Savior, it cannot be a holiday. For those of you who have gathered around the cross and have been saved and washed clean by His blood, it's a sacrilege to do anything else on that day except to celebrate what God has done.

If we abuse Sunday, we're going to destroy something beautiful that God has given. No Sunday means no church; no church means no worship; no worship means no religion; no religion means no morality; no morality means no society; no society means no government; no government means anarchy. That's the choice before us.

So, what do you do with the day? Do you sit around and read the Bible all day long? That might not be a bad idea for some of us. There are always those people who say, "I can worship God out on the golf course." Golf is a great sport, but it isn't worship! Those people who want to get out into God's great outdoors are God's great blue-domers. They're going to worship under the blue dome. But that isn't worship; it's recreation. Worship is when you're with the body of Christ.

Don't ever negate public worship, for something flows between us when we're together. Those who are full give to those who are empty; those who are thirsty come to get their cups filled. God is here; God's presence is among us, even though you don't hear thunder and lightning.

Here are some suggestions for the use of your Sabbath.

Worship: Real worship is not optional. You do not have to

decide each Sunday morning whether or not you'll worship; it should be programmed into your life.

Good conduct: It's a time when you should do things that are holy. If you do a little planning, you don't have to do your shopping on Sunday. There can be time to do things like that on other days. Remember that every day is His. We are not to give Him one day and do as we please the other six.

Be aware of your witness: What about your neighbor? Can he set his clock by the fact that your car pulls out of the driveway at a certain time on Sunday morning, and you're on your way to the worship of God? Don't forget the power of your witness; no man lives to himself, or dies to himself.

It's a day for family: A lot of families don't want this much time together. Many families are caught up with working and strained schedules. It needs to be a day for family and prayer and thinking. However you handle it — walking in the woods, doing something together as a family, or whatever — this should be done after you worship.

Prepare yourself: Do you pray for the pastor, your teacher, and the choir before you go to church? Do you prepare your mind and body ahead of time so that your spirit will be ready? God blesses in relationship to our preparation.

This is the day of rejoicing. Take this day as a gift from God and use it. It's not a burden to be imposed upon the people of God. It's a joy. It's God's answer to the mental health struggles of our day. This is God's great gift for us. Let us rejoice and be glad in it.

Prayer: *Dear Father, could it be that my depression and fatigue is my body demanding a Sabbath? My days are filled with stress, and I'm anxious about so many things. This week I will stop and catch up with myself. Even You, O God, rested after working six days. Why do I think I can defy Your plan for me? Quiet my soul as I prepare for the Sabbath – a holy day. Amen.*

REQUIREMENTS FOR COMMITMENT

61. Honor Your Parents (Commandment V)

Exodus 20:12 *"Honor your father and your mother, so that you may live long in the land the Lord your God is giving you."*

When God gave us the ten commandments, He made sure that the first four established our relationship to God. Now we turn to the six commandments dealing with man's relationship to man.

It is interesting that the bridge between our relationship to God and our relationship to our brother is the family bridge. We cross over the family bridge to find out how to relate to other people. In American life, we have come to a point where we don't think the family is as important as it used to be. We're finding all kinds of substitutes for family, and in the midst of this, families are breaking down. We're finding fathers against children, mothers against fathers, children against children, and no one seems to know what to do about it.

The commandment says, "Honor your father and your mother." In the New Testament, we receive these instructions: "Fathers, do not exasperate your children; instead, bring them up in the training and instruction of the Lord." (Ephesians 6:4). Many times this is a matter of improving communication and learning to understand each other at a deeper level.

One night, in the middle of the night, our doorbell rang, and there at the door was a young lady who was terribly distraught. We sat down with her in the family room and, as we listened to her, it became clear that the whole basis of her problem was that she and her father were just not communicating. Several days later, her father called. He didn't know the daughter had been to see us, and he wanted to talk about his heartbreak over her. He felt he had tried every way he could to reach her, but they just didn't speak the same language. The father was standing on one island trying to reach his daughter, and the daughter was standing on her own island trying to reach her father, but they couldn't find each other. There was no hatred; they just never could connect with one another.

A number of years ago, a family had gone to the mountains of North Carolina for their summer vacation. One of the young boys had his motorcycle with him, and he was enjoying riding it on the mountain roads. One night he went down the mountain, into the little village, for a date. The time passed more quickly than he realized. He started up the mountain as fast as he could. The parents were worried about the boy being so late, so the father got in the car to go look for him. As the boy was coming up the mountain, his father was going down. They came to the same curve at the same time, collided, and the boy was killed. The father will have a living death for the rest of his life.

That's what seems to be going on in our homes — people are running into each other. People who love one another are trying to find each other, standing on two separate islands. Or people are trying to get together by pulling in the wrong way, and running head-on into one another.

It's a sad thing that we don't have supports for the home any more.

Today we live in sprawling metropolises, where it's hard to keep a sense of community. We can't depend upon the schools or the entertainment media to reinforce our values, so families find themselves having to go against the mainstream of American life just to keep their family together. We've specialized not in preventive medicine, where the family is held together, but in emergency medicine.

The scripture says the way to pull it back together is simple — parents are to be honored. What does the word "honored" mean? Does it mean flowers on Mother's Day, or a tie on Father's Day? Does it mean coming home at Christmas? Does it mean a visit every now and then? Somehow it's gotten twisted.

Prayer: *Think of some families you know who are having problems, and pray for them by name. (This is the best help you can give.) Pray for your own family by name – your parents and extended family, as well as your immediate family. Ask God to bless our homes. Amen.*

REQUIREMENTS FOR COMMITMENT

62. Mode of Honor (Commandment V)

Ephesians 6:1-3 *"Children, obey your parents in the Lord, for this is right. 'Honor your father and mother' – which is the first commandment with a promise – 'that it may go well with you, and that you may enjoy long life on the earth.'"*

The word honor is the exact opposite of the word vain, which means to make empty. Its meaning is heaviness. You shall put all your weight down on honoring parents. It's the word for value, because value was conceived in those days in the weight of gold. "Make heavy" or "make valuable" meant to put weight and value in your relationship with your parents.

Interestingly enough, the breakdown of all civilizations began with the breakdown of the home. The Romans had a great family life, until they conquered Greece. The Greeks had a family life that was not as strong and stable as the Romans'. The Romans conquered Greece, and then the Greek morality conquered the Romans. The Romans returned home, with the moral values of the Greeks, and they both fell.

What does it mean to honor parents? To honor a parent means that you pay attention to them. Senior adults deserve to be listened to. The Chinese culture has something to teach us here, for the Chinese honor the old. They realize that each generation does not start over and stand on its own, but it learns from the previous generations. They need to be listened to, for they have a great deal to tell us. Listening to the old does not mean simply sitting around and letting them spin their yarns; it means an intimacy that says, "I value your opinion."

You honor a parent by giving them your time. About the time children reach puberty, our families splinter. Teen-agers have their thing, adults have their thing, and everybody goes their own way. There needs to be an investment of time. There needs to be a time when everyone is together — dinner, breakfast, or whatever. We made a rule in our family that drives everybody crazy, but we like it. We will not be apart from one another for more than forty-eight hours. Sometimes it may have to be a phone call, but we are in touch with each other. I know that's not possible for everyone, but it's been enriching for us. We make time for one another. Take that rule and decide that you're going to spend time with parents, with one another, with children.

Parents also are honored when children accept their values of thrift, worship, and integrity — values that survive the long haul. Parents need to feel, see, and hear an explicit expression of your love. Some of the saddest people are parents whose children will not make an effort to come to see them.

Honor your parents by establishing a home that reflects the values with which you grew up. Nothing will make a parent happier than to see his adult children making sure that grandchildren are nurtured in a warm, loving environment, and that they have significant religious training and opportunities for worship.

Prayer: *Father, I pray for patience and understanding in relating to my parents. Show me ways that I can express love and gratitude to them. Most of all, let me live the kind of life that will bring joy and pleasure – not embarrassment – to them. Give me the grace to be generous with time and expressions of love. Amen.*

REQUIREMENTS FOR COMMITMENT

63. Right to Life (Commandment VI)

Genesis 1:27 *So God created man in His own image, in the image of God He created him, male and female He created them.*

Exodus 20:13 *"You shall not murder."*

Murder is a word that has become more and more common in our day. We like to think that we are too civilized for murder to be of any concern to us, but unfortunately that's not the case.

One Sunday morning after a church staff meeting, a staff member came back down the hall with a very distraught young lady in her late twenties. She was disheveled and obviously had been up most of the night. Her husband had threatened to kill her, and there had been a violent struggle. She said she came to church because she knew he would not kill her there. As we talked, she said he might come looking for her. She handed over her purse. Inside there was a .38 revolver. We talked until she was somewhat calmer, and then we found someone who could help her. But the experience provided the obvious text for that day: "You shall not murder."

The commandment clearly says that human life is special. All over the Eastern world, human life was considered to be something that was cheap and to be thrown away. God came to His people and said it is sacred. He said, you shall not take up a club and kill another man, and if your ox gores another man, it's your responsibility. If a dead man was found halfway between two cities, the people always tried to determine which city he was closest to, so they would know which was responsible for his death.

Perhaps this is where we need to emphasize the responsibility of people who drive while intoxicated and kill the innocent. And don't forget about the drug user, who kills his brain to the point that he is oblivious to acts of crime.

You say, "I have done none of these things. I would never kill anyone." Perhaps we should stop at the end of each day and consider, "Have I killed my fellow man today with hatred? Is he a dead weight at the bottom of my heart?" We need to understand that human life is very precious in the eyes of God. We can never approach the question of taking human life casually.

94

Prayer: *"O Lord, You have searched me, and You know me. You know when I sit and when I rise; You perceive my thoughts from afar. You discern my going out and my lying down; You are familiar with all my ways." (Psalm 139:1-3) You love me even with all my evil ways, O Lord. Purify my thoughts and my life, so that in no way will I murder one of Your dear children. Amen.*

REQUIREMENTS FOR COMMITMENT

64. Dial A (Anger) for Murder (Commandment VI)

Matthew 5:21, 22 *"You have heard it was said to the people long ago, 'Do not murder, and anyone who murders will be subject to judgment.' But I tell you that anyone who is angry with his brother will be subject to judgment. Again, anyone who says to his brother, 'Raca,' is answerable to the Sanhedrin. But anyone who says, 'You fool,' will be in danger of the fire of hell."*

This commandment talks about murder. Most of us carry the most deadly weapon concealed in our mouths — the tongue. We use this part of our anatomy as a deadly weapon when anger takes control. Do you know what Jesus talks about as the root of our killing? He talks about taking excessive anger and putting it on someone else, or dealing with another person as though he is a fool. The word "raca" was a slang expression of that day. Jesus said, if you deal with your brother as though he is of no consequence, if you call him raca or fool, then you've killed him.

Anger is something that everybody understands. You can let your anger flow unchecked, and people will stand aside and allow that it is the human way. But we have destroyed more people with our unleashed anger than we ever have with guns in our hands.

There is a classic story in the eighteenth-century novel, *The Days of Our Years*. In a small French village, there is a very low income family with two children. One is a hunchback boy; the other is a girl. The father dies and the mother is very sick. The boy is accused falsely of a crime and sent to prison, leaving his sister to do what she can to support their mother; the young girl becomes a prostitute. When the boy gets out of prison, he walks down the main street of his village, and all the town ruffians come out and taunt him about his sister. He is so humiliated that he goes down to the river and drowns himself. The next night, the grief-stricken girl takes a gun and kills herself. The whole village attends the funeral of these two children. The priest, who is incensed by all of this, says, "These were not suicides; these children did not kill themselves. Christian, when the Lord of life and death shall ask me on the day of judgment, 'Where are thy sheep?' I shall not answer him. When the Lord asks me a second time, 'Pastor, where are thy sheep?' I shall answer him this way. 'Lord, I have no sheep; they are a pack of wolves.'"

We legitimatize the one thing that Jesus said destroys human personality. We legitimatize anger when it's used against other people. Jesus said, "I have come that you may have life;" He was a life giver. Everywhere He went, people flocked around Him because He gave life. Your anger takes life away.

Those of you who are angry with your children, in-laws, husband, or wife, remember that this anger cuts away life. Some of you have found pet things to put your anger on. You're angry with the government, this movement or that; you're angry with the church, your pastor, or your deacon. But Jesus didn't come to legitimatize that kind of anger; Jesus came that you may have life.

See the great contrast between life and death that's in the gospel. Jesus brings life; the world brings death.

The commandment talks about murder. It prohibits us from destruction of life, but we go on another step and understand that it provides, in Jesus Christ, *for* life. You know it is wrong to take a gun and shoot somebody. Go one step further and be a life-giver. It won't hurt you to say good things, to be supportive.

Once there was a girl who worked in a poison garden. She was a beautiful maiden, but after a while, the poisons from that garden came into her life and made her very ugly. Eventually, anything she touched died. That's the way parts of the world are today. That's the kind of disease that some people have. It's a disease of anger that makes things die. You say you're afraid of love, that it's too free and open and flexible in this crazy world. We dare you to pray for the gift of love. Let God burn the anger out.

Prayer: *Father, I pray that anger will not control my thoughts and actions any longer. It does keep me from being a positive influence. Let me express love and affirmation instead of anger. Amen.*

REQUIREMENTS FOR COMMITMENT

65. Never Take a Fence Down Until . . . (Commandment VII)

Exodus 20:14 *"You shall not commit adultery."*
Matthew 5:27, 28 *"You have heard that it was said, 'Do not commit adultery.' But I tell you that anyone who looks at a woman lustfully has already commited adultery with her in his heart."*

There is an old saying that goes, "Never take down a fence until you know why the fence was put up." There is a sanctity of the human relationship that transcends anything we can imagine. The Bible talks about crimes against life, against property, and against marriage. It has been the accumulated wisdom of the generations that the sexual relationship between male and female in marriage is a divine relationship, and a sexual relationship outside of marriage is a sacrilege. God says that your family is holy, and He says that the relationship between male and female is so holy that it parallels the covenant made between Israel and God at Sinai.

In the New Testament, Paul says the same thing. He says that the relationship between a man and his bride is the same as the relationship between Christ and his church. The Bible does not put the kind of restrictions on us that take away the joy of life, but it tells us the way God intends for us to live. If we live God's way, we will have joy and fulfillment. The evil one has taken the things God has given us and perverted them. He has taken the power to get your adrenalin going and turned it into destructive anger. He has taken appetites and told us to eat anything we want, and has turned us into beasts or drunkards. God gave appetites and God gave drives and forces, but He also gave some fences to keep them hedged in, so they would do what they were made to do. He gave sexual drives. That is not only a biological relationship between male and female, but also a covenant between husband and wife — a covenant so important that it is made in the house of God and with His blessing. They have made a covenant of fidelity.

It's been several years since a young man and his girlfriend came to our home late one night to talk. They had tears running down their cheeks, as they told about their involvement in a sexual indiscretion. There was a great deal of repentance and asking for healing during the conversation, and they kept saying over and over again, "Why didn't somebody tell us?" What they did not realize was that they had been told time and time again about the relationship between male and female; how it was to be constructed, what it was about, and the sanctity of this relationship. As they talked about how everything they had seen and heard had not gotten through to them, they realized that they had violated what their parents and their church had been teaching them all this time. When they left, we were as grieved as they were, because no matter what we did to try to patch up the bad situation, we found that they had been scarred for a lifetime.

If you have secret sins and broken relationships and are burdened by guilt, listen to this good news. Read the eighth chapter of John, where Jesus, in talking to the woman taken in adultery, said, "Go and sin no more." Forgiveness and a direction are given. Jesus said that you can be clean and whole. The tone and thrust of the Bible is to put up the fence to let you know you're in danger if you break the covenantal relationship God has given you. But the kind of God revealed in the Bible, and in the person of Jesus Christ, is a God who forgives.

The Bible assumes we will remain faithful to our marital covenant. We were praying one time about some couples in our church whose family relationships were breaking down. We observed that if the parties in the marriages had spent as much time keeping their covenantal relationship together, and keeping their marriages alive, as they had on their affairs, their marriages would have been saved. We don't have an easy gimmick for you, but we do have an easy direction for you. If you have a choice between morality and immorality, choose morality, for immorality will be destructive and costly. Spend your time cultivating your marital relationship with your wife or husband. Spend some time growing and talking things through, for to break the bond that God made between you and your spouse is to break a covenant with God. You need to renew your vows and understand that the fence was put there to keep you from getting hurt. Don't take it down. The accumulated wisdom of the ages and the word of God is that the fence is there for a purpose.

If you're young, keep yourself clean. If you've gotten spotted by the world, pray for forgiveness. If there is a break in your marriage, pray for healing. If you find yourself having to put the pieces together again, pray for God's guidance. The main thing is to understand the implications of the seventh commandment — Thou shalt not commit adultery for your life, and for the life of your family under Christ.

Prayer: *Father, I know You have a purpose for my life. Please let me grow in wisdom and understanding. I pray for help with my relationships with my family. (If you are married, pray for your spouse. If you are single, pray for the strength to be the person God wants you to be.) Amen.*

REQUIREMENTS FOR COMMITMENT

66. What's Yours Is Mine (Commandment VIII)

Luke 10:29,30 *And who is my neighbor? . . . a man was going down from Jerusalem to Jericho when he fell into the hands of robbers . . .*

In this meditation, we want to think about property. There are clearly three views in the world. Jesus used a story about a man traveling from Jerusalem to Jericho to set the stage for His teaching. The man was robbed, stripped, beaten, and left for dead by the side of the road. Three groups of people came along, and their response to the poor man is the basis for the discussion on stealing and neighbors.

WHAT'S YOURS IS MINE. In this story, Jesus gives us a parable that shows the three basic attitudes toward wealth in our world. The first attitude we see in the thieves. When they came along, they said by their actions, "What's yours is mine, and I'm going to take it." They fell upon the man and stripped him of everything he had.

There are a lot of people in our world who have the "what's yours is mine" attitude about things. Their posture is that, if you have something they want, they can take it from you. St. Augustine said that stealing is to get another person's property wrongfully into our own possession.

The Christian faith is not at war with the use of property; it is not anti-material. God has given us a wholesome appreciation that He made the world, and the book of Genesis says, "It is good." That also means that man has a right to property, and we have no right to extract it from him in illegal ways. In our culture, we probably break this commandment more than any other. We somehow think that we have a right to take anything that's out in the public. A woman complains to her husband that the maid has stolen the towels they took from a hotel in London. A ship docked in New York Harbor was opened to the public for tours; when it was closed, the officials found that everything movable had been stripped from it. Two women were on a bus and one had forgotten to pay her fare. As they were going down the street, she said, "You know, I feel a little bad; I did not pay." The other one said, "Well, you don't need to feel bad about that, but actually honesty *does* pay. I paid my fare with a one-dollar bill and received change for a five!"

101

WHAT'S MINE IS MINE AND I'LL KEEP IT. This is the second basic attitude that Jesus described in the story about the man who was robbed. We probably see this more often than any other attitude in our culture. It is the idea that I own everything — my car, my house, my clothes — and I'll do as I please with it. But in truth, God owns everything, and the Christian is only a steward of this world. When God put man in the Garden of Eden, He made it crystal clear that man was only a caretaker, or steward, of the Garden. We have already legitimatized wealth and possession of property, but we must understand that we have to use it for a certain purpose, if we name Jesus Christ as Savior and Lord. We cannot rob God. If we take it for ourselves and say, "It is mine, and I'm going to keep it for myself," that is almost as bad as the thieves who violated another man. We have violated God and robbed him.

WHAT'S MINE IS YOURS, AND I'LL GIVE IT. This is the third view of property and wealth. The generous person is the one whom people admire and trust. Sin is basically pride; pride is self-ishness; selfishness is stealing. Our own greed stands in the way of greatness. We can become so involved in making sure that we get more than our share of everything, that we miss life's most meaning-ful gifts.

Remember how Jesus called Zaccheus out of the sycamore tree? Jesus affirmed this tax collector, who had stolen from his own people, and Zaccheus' heart was changed. He gave half his goods to the poor and returned anything he had taken falsely. When God gets into the heart, we worship God instead of things; our attitude about people and possessions changes, and we become generous. Only a thoughtful, caring, benevolent person can know true joy — the joy of giving.

Prayer: *Father, let me not be guilty of stealing from anyone. Let me be an example of a caring and generous person. Amen.*

REQUIREMENTS FOR COMMITMENT

67. To Tell the Truth (Commandment IX)

Exodus 20:16 *"You shall not give false testimony against your neighbor."*

Most of us probably feel that this is one commandment we don't have to worry about. Not many will be called on to go to court to witness against a neighbor. However, if we really study these words, we see that God didn't limit this commandment only to the court system. He also meant for us not to give false testimony against our neighbor in the normal transactions of life.

Jesus said, "For out of the overflow of the heart, the mouth speaks." God intends for us to be truthful in our relationship to Him and to our fellow man.

Do you remember the night when Peter had denied the Lord three times and was under great stress? A maid came into Peter's presence and said, "You're a follower of Jesus of Nazareth. I know you because your tongue betrays you." Speech may betray you, too. Jesus said, ". . . men will have to give account on the day of judgment for every careless word spoken. For by your words you will be acquitted and by your words you will be condemned." (Matthew 12:36, 37)

Go to an educator, talk to him for five minutes, and he'll tell you what you've read and how far you've gone in school. Go to a doctor, and he can tell you about your health. Go to a psychiatrist, and he'll tell you what's going on in those deep recesses of your life. You see, your speech doesn't cover up; it betrays what is inside.

The tongue has a very positive power. The Hebrews knew the power of speech. Can't you imagine them sitting around the campfire every night, telling stories about how they had walked across the desert? The storyteller would give the background on how it had been down in Egypt, what the taskmaster's lashes had felt like across his back, and what it was like to make bricks without straw. Those who understand the Hebrew mind say that a good storyteller made words jump into the fire, leap out at people, and then dance around the fire. They understood the power of words.

Indeed, words are more powerful than armies, for words command armies. Words are more powerful than machinery, for words command machinery. Life and death are in the power of the tongue.

The Bible says that nothing happened until God spoke. We

think that's some kind of cryptic, marvelous, romantic insight into the creation of the earth. Nothing happened until out of the heart of God came a word. "In the beginning was the word, and the word was God, and the word was with God, and God spoke." God put the word out, and the heavens and the earth, the firmament and the water, all came together. What do we preach? We preach the *Word* of God. What did Jesus do? He died, but we spend our lives understanding what He *said*. Don't negate the power of the Word, for the Scriptures tell us that the Word of God — the heart of God articulated out of the soul of God — became flesh. Jesus is the Word of God's flesh moving among us.

The tongue, however, does have its destructive power. Unless the tongue is yielded to God, it is an unruly evil. The tongue defiles the whole body. Few men seem to tame it. Job says it is a scourge. The Psalmist says, "Their throats are open graves." "With the tongue we praise our Lord and Father, and with it we curse men, who have been made in God's likeness. Out of the same mouth come praise and cursing." (James 3:9,10)

Prayer: *Dear Father, please help me to be careful of the words that come from my mouth. Give me a clean and pure heart, so that the words that flow out will be a blessing to You and man, and not a curse. Amen.*

REQUIREMENTS FOR COMMITMENT

68. Sticks and Stones Versus Words (Commandment IX)

James 4:11a *"Brothers, do not slander one another. Anyone who speaks against his brother or judges him, speaks against the law and judges it."*
James 5:9 *"Don't grumble against each other, brothers, or you will be judged."*

We have three levels of conversation. The lowest level is when you talk about people. "Did you hear what I heard about. . . . " The second level of conversation is when you talk about things — new cars, new clothes, new televisions, new houses. The highest level is when you talk about ideas.

The destructive power of the tongue has had its mark upon history. The gossiping tongue has destroyed reputations, and the lying tongue has done incredible damage to people. Joseph, sold into slavery by his brothers, was hurt more by the lying tongue of Potipher's wife. Moses, when he took the Ethiopian woman as his wife in the book of Numbers, had to put up with the chiding and the gossip of Miriam and Aaron. David, when he went out to fight Goliath, had to listen to the giant's taunting and making fun of him and his God. Paul said the tongues of the philosphers were worse to him than all the whips that he had endured.

Some people are skilled in saying good things but meaning evil. William Law, in *A Sincere Call to a Devout and Holy Life*, talks about people who have a thread of candor, but weave it with a web of lies. Shakespeare must have known more about language than we ever understood, for he said, "He who steals my purse steals trash, but he who filches from me my good name, robs me of that which enriches not him and makes me poor, indeed."

The first atomic bomb had a mechanism in the heart of it which was the size of a golf ball. The bomb itself was huge, but the small mechanism that made the difference equalled five million, four hundred thousand pounds of TNT. The tongue is just as small, but it has the same kind of power as that bomb. Connect that kind of power to something of value, and good things happen. But let that power run amuck, and it causes destruction.

The speaker who preceded Abraham Lincoln at Gettysburg spoke for an hour and a half. Then Lincoln gave a three-minute speech that changed the course of American history, and began to heal the wounds of the nation. Henry Grady, the son of the city of Atlanta, was able to unite the North and the South through his oratory and writing.

Historians tell us that, had it not been for John Wesley and his dedication to the gospel, the French Revolution would have spread to England. Had the tongue of John Wesley not been set on fire by the Spirit of God, England would have gone through a political revolution rather than a spiritual revolution. The hearts of men were changed and England was saved.

What about you? The commandment says to speak the truth. We need to ask God to give us a clean heart. We are not going to speak good words out of a dirty heart. You may put perfume on a sewer, but it's still a sewer. We must learn to let our words put men on their feet. Reach out with your language and touch other people. Give them grace and strength, send them on their way, and let them feel the stroke of God's affirmation by your tongue. Let them know that the words you speak are true and honest and healing.

Prayer: *Dear Father, teach me to speak healing words. Let me not be afraid to say, "I love you," "I appreciate you," "You are O.K.," and "Thank you." I pray that my tongue will not maim or destroy another person. Let me speak the truth in love. Amen.*

REQUIREMENTS FOR COMMITMENT

69. Covetousness (Commandment X)

Exodus 20:17 *"You shall not covet your neighbor's house. You shall not covet your neighbor's wife, or his manservant or maidservant, his ox or donkey, or anything that belongs to your neighbor."*
Matthew 6:33 *"But seek first His kingdom and His righteousness, and all these things will be given to you as well."*

The dictionary definition for the word "covet" is, to desire inordinately or without due regard for the rights of others; desire wrongfully.

Covetousness is really a disease of the spirit, because it is an action which comes from inside a person. Desire isn't bad; it's only when we become greedy and grasping that we are afflicted with the disease of covetousness.

What causes this disease of inordinate desire? Just being human can be the cause. The Israelites didn't have the influences on them that we have today, but they obviously had the problem.

Perhaps the biggest cause of the disease is living in an affluent society. Living among people who seem to have so much elevates the desire of less fortunate people to an unhealthy degree. Television commercials taunt many people, and desire quickly becomes covetousness.

What are the symptoms? How do you know if you are coming down with a bad case of covetousness? You'll feel palpitations of the pocketbook. It will be very difficult to walk through a shopping center and not buy something, whether you need it or not. A sign of maturity is to have money in your pocket and not have to spend it.

Why did God mention coveting your neighbor's house? The Israelites had only tents. Maybe the Bible is more relevant than we think. Have you ever envied and even been covetous of your neighbor's move to a bigger house in a better neighborhood? What about his brand-new car? Or your neighbor's cute, sweet wife or handsome husband? How can they afford that new boat?

Another symptom of this disease is spiritual myopia. Your vision will be cut, and all you will ask is, how much does it cost? It is sad and dangerous when a person or group measures everything by what it costs.

The third symptom is the feeling of separation from God. No man can serve two masters. You can't serve worldly possessions and God, too. The more our desires become avaricious and unhealthy, the greater the feeling of separation from God and the things of His kingdom.

What is the course of this disease? What will it do? Quite bluntly and simply, it will kill you. Misdirected desires bring death of the spirit. You will become so calloused and hardened to the needs of the world, that soon you won't feel anything at all. You will be a walking dead person.

Is there a cure for covetousness? It can be cured, but it takes a strong commitment to Jesus Christ. Seek first the kingdom of God and stand firm. Rededicate your life to good action (righteousness), desire that people everywhere hear the word of God. Desire adventure for your life. Let God use you for something good. Express a healthy witness for Jesus.

God recognized the dangers of the disease of covetousness. He knew it is like a cancer, that eats away at the soul of a person so afflicted. He said, "Do not covet." Jesus added, "Seek first the kingdom of God, and all these things will be given to you."

Prayer: *Father, it is so hard to avoid being covetous. Sometimes it seems like everybody has more of everything than I do. It hurts me. Help me keep my mind on the truly important things – Your kingdom. Let me do my part to make Your kingdom come on earth. Amen.*

THE DARKNESS WHERE GOD WAS

70. Are You There, God?

Exodus 20:21 *The people remained at a distance, while Moses approached the thick darkness where God was.*

After Moses had delivered the ten commandments to the people at the foot of Mount Sinai, they trembled in fear as they saw the thunder and lightning, heard the trumpet, and observed the mountain in smoke. Then Moses withdrew from the people and approached the darkness where God was.

You need to have a mental picture of the Sinai Peninsula and the mountain in order to understand what the people were experiencing. Someone has said that the Sinai Peninsula is twenty-four thousand square miles of nothingness. It is usually written off as little more than desert, wilderness, and mountains. We journeyed to Sinai on the coldest day in fifty years. The desert had snow on it, and as we climbed to the top of Mount Sinai, we slid on the ice. Sinai looks much like you would expect a desert to look, except for the red rock that emerges from it. There is a cove cut back into the rock. In the middle of that cove is a place that is said to be where Aaron built the altar to the golden calf, and where Moses broke the tablets. Behind that is a monastery that is fourteen hundred years old and is the second greatest repository of christian writings and history on earth. Behind the monastery is the Mount of St. Catherine, and then there is the towering Mount Sinai.

To see this is an overpowering experience. When God led Moses to bring the children of Israel out of bondage, they came across the Red Sea, went down the Sinai Peninsula, then turned and came over to this mountain. They were brought into the cove that goes back into the mountain, with the shadow of Sinai coming upon them. Moses left the people and climbed the craggy mountain, rock by rock. It must have taken him days to get to the top, for Sinai goes seven thousand, four hundred two feet above sea level. There at the top of that mountain, in the quietness of the moment, God spoke to him. When he came down, he found the people caught in revelry, and was so disgusted with them that he broke the tablets and went back up the mountain.

Seven times Moses went up and down that mountain, but in this particular passage, when Moses came down, he read the commandments to the people. This was to be the law of the people of Israel, and, as he read it to them, the people were astonished because a cloud came over the top of Mount Sinai. We believe what the Bible says is true — the presence of God was there in that thick cloud that hovered over the mountain. Even centuries after that great experience, there is a sense of the presence of God there. After Moses had read the commandments, he turned and went back up into the cloud, into the darkness where God was.

It is overwhelming for us to come into some very difficult places in life, because they seem to be so dark. You think that because life has become dark, God has abandoned you. But it is in the cloud of life that God is most vivid. It is in the deep places, the hard, difficult, agonizing places of life, where God walks the strongest. That is the message of the book of Exodus. In our pilgrimage, all along the way, God is there in the dark places.

Your eyes show the burdens you carry, the crises you are up against. Your heart is aching beneath all the smooth-polished exterior you show. Most people carry a broken heart around, but we know out of the experience of our own lives that God is in the dark cloud. You can know that he is true and faithful, because the Bible declares it, human experience affirms it, and personal revelation sanctifies it.

Prayer: *Rescue me, Lord, from the darkness I am in. I don't know what will happen to me and my family. I feel very alone, so isolated. Let me say with the Psalmist: "Though I walk in the midst of trouble, You preserve my life; You stretch out Your hand against the anger of my foes, with Your right hand You save me. The Lord will fulfill His purpose for me; Your love, O Lord, endures forever. Do not abandon the works of Your hands." (Psalm 138:7,8) Amen.*

THE DARKNESS WHERE GOD WAS

71. The Darkness of Sin

Psalm 18:16,17 *He reached down from on high and took hold of me; He drew me out of deep waters. He rescued me from my powerful enemy, from my foes, who were too strong for me.*

Exodus 20:21b . . . . *Moses approached the thick darkness where God was.*

There is another darkness — the darkness of human sin. After walking through the ancient world again, we are convinced that man has not learned a new way to sin in five thousand years. Anything the ancients did, we do; and anything that we do, the ancients did before us. But today, we seem to promote sin more than ever before; we try to erase the black and white of the world to make it gray.

Young adults get caught in this trap. They have listened to the serpent's voice, and they have been lured by him. They have been told by the serpent that he will make them wiser and smarter, only to find that he has destroyed them. Some young couples have taken the poison of our culture and squeezed it and let it run into their lives, only to find that the dead philosophies of our culture are the serpent's poison.

Others, in their middle years, get tired of walking the straight and narrow. They throw it all away, saying they're going to have one last fling, only to find that it damages and destroys. And some have let the slow poison of bad attitudes get in and cloud the very essence of life. All of a sudden, like Simon Peter, you sit by the fire of the enemy warming your hands, denying your Lord.

It isn't pleasant to be reminded that some of our darkness is our own doing. It isn't pleasant to realize that none of us is spotless, that all of us have sinned and come short of the glory of God.

Our Lord knows that. He is sinless, yet He bore our sins. He is perfect, yet He bore our imperfection. Somebody may look at you and say that your garments are stained, but our Lord looks at you and says, "Yes, but I'll make them clean." You don't need to stay the way you are. The sin is trying to make you stay that way, but Jesus says you can be clean.

In the midst of the dark places where you live, God is there. Whatever that darkness may be, the darkness of your own personal sin, you are not big and strong enough, or creative and powerful enough, to commit a sin that God can't cure. Jesus will wash you clean; He'll pull you out of that darkness. Jesus will give you light where there has been darkness.

The trouble is that too many people have become accustomed to their sin, and like it that way, and don't want to be made clean. We get used to our filth and the darkness of sin. God's love brought the light to our darkness. Despite our sinful ways, God will not abandon us. He will cleanse, heal and protect His children.

Prayer: *Lord, deliver me from evil. As humans, we are so vulnerable and inadequate to meet the dangers in our path. I deliver myself to Your protecting power . . . power in the darkness. Amen.*

THE DARKNESS WHERE GOD WAS

72. The Darkness of Death

Psalm 23:1,4 *The Lord is my shepherd, I shall lack nothing. . . . Even though I walk through the valley of the shadow of death, [the darkest valley], I will fear no evil, for you are with me.*

There is another darkness where God is — the darkness of death. We don't like to talk about it. A lot of people get uneasy when we say even the word "death." We're supposed to say "passed away" or "gone to his reward." For many of us, death is not a part of our lives; we don't really acknowledge that it exists, because we prefer to believe that we're going to live forever. Just take a look at the cosmetics counter; everything there is designed to make you look tall, skinny, and twenty-one.

But we must face death.

The Bible says there is the valley of the shadow, and it is that shadow — the unknown — which scares most people. We don't know what's out there, and we're frightened about it. We've warmed our hands at the enemy's fire so long, and we are so stained by the scent and so scorched by the smoke of that fire, that we don't want to go through death.

We'd like to believe the words of the preacher, who talks about people living forever — spiritual bodies — but the darkness is frightening. But God has given power over death to the Christian.

In Jesus Christ, we have been given the *power* of the resurrection. The experience makes it possible for a Christian to enter the darkness of the tomb and never be frightened. We shall live forever, with spiritual bodies and recognizable personages. But as we live forever, we live with Him, because Jesus went into the darkness ahead of us. As Moses went up to the holy mountain into the darkness to face God, so Jesus has gone into the darkness of the tomb, to give us deliverance from the fear and stain of death.

"If a man be in Christ, he is a new creature." If you confess that Jesus is Lord, and believe in your heart that God raised Him from the dead, you will be saved. (Romans 10:9)

"Everyone who calls on the name of the Lord will be saved." (Romans 10:13)

Prayer: *Think about yourself and what your darkness is. Are you in the darkness of bitterness or hatred? Are you feeling separated? Are you floundering? Pray about these areas of darkness. Now decide to become a part of a caring community of faith – church. Now pray for peace and calm in your soul. Amen.*

THE PATHWAY UPWARD

73. Keep Moving On Up

Exodus 24:1 *Then He said to Moses, "Come on up to the Lord, you and Aaron, Nadab and Abihu and seventy of the elders of Israel."*

There were a million or so people assembled at the bottom of Mount Sinai, and out of them God called a select few. The masses of people at the bottom of the mountain probably didn't care what happened at the top of that mountain. They were not too concerned about what God was saying to Moses, or what God was doing with the elders. All they wanted to know was, "Are we going to be able to eat? Are we going to have enough to live on? Is everything going my way?"

Years ago, when we lived in a south Florida community, we made some interesting observations of how some people used church functions for their own profit. We had a covered dish supper once a week, and there were many there who never came any other time. They would go down the line, heaping food on their plates, and after supper was over, they wouldn't stay for the prayer service. They'd just leave, and we wouldn't see them again until the next Wednesday night. One man said they had heard that our church had the best deal in town on Wednesday night, and they were coming from the trailer park to eat supper! We were glad to have them visit with us, but when we mentioned the possibility of their becoming involved and committed to the church, they said they had no intention of doing so.

Some people let others put the commitment in, and they take the commitment out. They let other people make the hard decisions, and they do the fun things. Their idea is to let other people really keep it together, but they want the church to serve them, and they want God at their beck and call. The masses at the bottom of the mountain are getting all the good they can out of it, putting nothing back into it, and complaining when any demand is made upon their lives. This is true also with family life. In some instances, either father or mother refuses to accept normal responsibilities concerning the welfare of the household. Sometimes the children expect to reap the benefits of the family without carrying their share of the load. A lot of family members are eating at the table without providing anything themselves.

God has a plan for you and your family; He has great plans for your church, but you'll never know what they are as long as you're content to be with the masses at the bottom of the mountain. Where is your commitment? Are you at the bottom of the mountain with the crowd? Do you take the sacrament in the morning and commit sacrilege at night? Is it a matter of saying "hosanna" in the early part of the week and "crucify Him" at the end? It takes courage to step up and away from the crowd. They will be sure to try to intimidate you and your family, because you are brave and exhibit faith and faithfulness. Bring your covered dish to the table full of nourishing food, and joyfully participate in God's plans for you and His kingdom.

Prayer: *Father, cure my inertia, my half-hearted participation in Your kingdom's plan. Give me strength in the inner being and courage to move on up and away from the masses at the bottom of the mountain. Amen.*

THE PATHWAY UPWARD

74. Come to the Table

Exodus 24:5,9,10,11 *Then he sent young Israelite men, and they offered burnt offerings and sacrificed young bulls as fellowship offerings to the Lord. Exodus 24:5*
Moses and Aaron, Nadab and Abihu, and the seventy elders of Israel went up and saw the God of Israel. Under His feet was something like a pavement made of sapphire, clear as the sky itself. But God did not raise His hand against these leaders of Israel; they saw God, and they ate and drank. Exodus 24:9,10,11

Do you ever wish that you could have one of those dramatic religious experiences that some people have and tell the world about? Do you ever wonder, "What is wrong with me?" when testimony time comes and you have nothing spectacular to tell? Well, look at what happened to Aaron, his two sons, and the seventy elders. God called them to another level — a plateau above the masses at the foot of Mount Sinai. A marvelous thing occurred on this plateau. They obeyed the Lord and made a sacrifice. They took the blood of the sacrifice and sprinkled half of it over the seventy, and the other half they symbolically sprinkled over the people. Then in the midst of that experience, there seemed to be a breakthrough of religious encounter. The heavens opened and they saw the very presence of the Lord God.

The scripture says that they ate and drank. It sounds like a picnic in the presence of God on the mountain of God. We have opportunities for supper with God and usually don't accept the invitation. We don't recognize the invitation, because we aren't tuned in to the ways of God. Experiences with God come from living in an attitude of expectation, of understanding His ways. Well, the moment of ecstasy was short-lived because, soon after that, the infamous golden calf came into being.

God doesn't give religious ecstasy for the sake of having ecstasy. He gives religious knowledge, vision, and ecstasy so that it can make a difference in your life. Some people go around and gather religious ecstasy as they gather flowers to be displayed somewhere, but God doesn't give ecstasy for that reason. He gives it to impower us to do something. If the seventy elders had had the right kind of religious experience, there never would have been the golden calf. What do you think was in the mind of Aaron when the mob came and said, build us a calf? Do you think he ever looked back and said, "I've seen God and He will sustain us and be with us." No, he just threw in. What happened on the mountain did not carry over.

Perhaps you had an experience early in your life, and you knew that you were spared for a purpose. Maybe your experience occurred during the illness or death of a relative or close friend. Perhaps the birth of your child heightened your awareness of the presence of God in your life, and you vowed that you'd never be the same again. But has it made any difference? When you came back to God's table to eat, did you eat any differently? Did it make any difference in your life?

God laid His hand on the elders of Israel to annoint them. He annointed them for a purpose, and they did not fulfill that purpose. God has opened up His heavens to us and we have looked in — we've seen the sapphire sea — but then it's back to the mundane business as usual. When God lays His hands on you and annoints you, ask His guidance to allow you to follow through and fulfill His purpose in your life.

Prayer: *Father, let me recognize the invitations You extend to Your table. I want to experience Your annointing in my life. Give me the power to fulfill Your purpose. Amen.*

THE PATHWAY UPWARD

75. Have I Got a Plan for You!

Exodus 24:12,13 *The Lord said to Moses, "Come up to me on the mountain and stay here, and I will give you the tablets of stone . . ." Then Moses set out with Joshua, his aide, and Moses went up the mountain of God.*
Jeremiah 29:11 *"For I know the plans I have for you," declares the Lord, "plans to prosper you and not to harm you, plans to give you hope and a future."*

God sometimes does great things through very young and inexperienced people. There are many people with extraordinary talents and skills, and God calls them to move on up out of the masses. Actually there are many average people who, because they are open to God's call, are used in unusual ways. God saw in Joshua, for example, a promising helper for Moses and a future leader of the people. God took Joshua to a level where he could mature and finely tune his life to the ways of God. Moses went on up the mountain, but Joshua had to stay behind to mature.

We've seen a lot of people, fresh from their first religious retreat, who try to dictate how everything at church should be done. Usually they observe that no one is "spiritual" enough. We cannot live without religious ecstasy. We cannot live without the vision of God. But we have to be willing to study and work and pray, and allow God to mature us for His purpose.

Many people are called to go on up the mountain, but they are too busy doing their own thing, or they say, "I might not want to do what God has in mind." But God will prepare you for whatever He has planned for you.

We have had a number of people listen to God's call to mission work, both at home and abroad. Some are doing short-term service of six months or a year. One young lady took a leave of absence from her company and spent a year helping to revitalize missionary work in Uganda. This experience seemed to be very intimidating to the people around her at work, in her apartment building, and even at church. Some said it would be ruining her career; others said she was wasting herself, throwing herself away. She said the intimidation became almost hostile as they said these things to her, trying to keep her from going. It simply was too much religious commitment for a lot of people to take. People are afraid of what God can do with them.

The reason the elders stayed where they did was that they were afraid to go up to the next level. They didn't know what God had for them. When Joshua went up to that level, he didn't know that God was preparing him to lead the people. When Moses was called on to the top, he didn't know what God had for him either, but he knew *who* was calling: the Lord God.

If you are not resting easily in your Christian commitment, it is because you don't trust God with your life. You are still hanging around the masses at the foot of the mountain. Move up to the plateau. Start climbing to the top. God does have a plan for you!

Prayer: *Father, give me a vision and the maturity to discern Your will for my life. Don't let career, family, friends, or my own desires get in the way of Your plan for me. Amen.*

VOICES OF OUR DAY

76. The Sound of Revelry

Exodus 32:15-18 *Moses turned and went down the mountain with the two tablets of the testimony in his hands. . . . The tablets were the work of God. . . . When Joshua heard the noise of the people shouting, he said to Moses, "There is the sound of war in the camp;" Moses replied, "It is not the sound of victory; it is not the sound of defeat; it is the sound of singing that I hear."*

Moses and Joshua had been on a long pilgrimage. As you know, Moses had been on top of the mountain for forty days and forty nights with the Lord, receiving the Ten Commandments. Joshua went almost to the top of the mountain with Moses, but not quite; he lingered back in a special place to wait for Moses' return. Joshua was a man who had military genius, and was in the forefront of protecting the children of Israel as they went into battle. Now the great time of inspiration was over. Those forty days had passed, and Moses was coming back with the law of God to give the people. It was paramount among the holy times in all of Israel's history.

Moses came down that long, craggy trail from the top of the mountain, stepping from rock to rock, and there he found Joshua waiting for him. We don't know where Joshua waited, but there is a valley called the Valley of Elijah near the top of Mount Sinai where it could have been. You can imagine that Moses came to him, took him by the arm, and started down the mountain again. As they neared the camp, they began to hear the noise of the people. Two men who had been away for forty days and forty nights should have been excited about hearing the sounds of their people, but that wasn't the case.

As they neared the camp, they heard "singing" (which was the word for revelry), and found the masses worshiping the golden calf. The people, in only forty days and nights, had tired of waiting (sound familiar?) and probably said, "Moses who?" or "God who?"

God told Moses what they were doing. He was so angry that Moses had to intervene and plead for the people. Perhaps Moses hoped that by the time he and Joshua got back to camp, Aaron would have straightened things out. Not so. "Moses saw that the people were running wild, and that Aaron had let them get out of control and so became a laughingstock to their enemies." (Exodus 34:25)

Can you imagine the disappointment and anger of Moses? You've probably known the humiliation and disappointment of seeing a loved one play the fool. Can you imagine how God must feel about us? We're supposed to be sophisticated and a long way from the debauchery of Israel and the golden calf, but we seem to have lost control of ourselves. We are quick to forget the voice of God, if He doesn't answer us quickly enough. It's easier to hear the voices of revelry and debauchery. They are awfully loud.

Prayer: *Forgive me, Lord, when I refuse to hear Your voice. (List some things you need to change in your life.) Help me to be a person who is strong like Moses. Amen.*

VOICES OF OUR DAY

77. Noise of Our Lives

Proverbs 19:20 *Listen to advice and accept instruction, and in the end, you will be wise.*

All of us have the ability to listen. Some of us can hear more than others, but everybody is caught up in the listening process in this world. Although we live on one of the busiest streets in Atlanta, with hundreds of cars passing all the time, we know the distinct sound of our son's little Volkswagen. Mothers who hear their babies cry in the middle of the night can tell instantly whether it's a cry of pain, or hunger, or just a call for attention. The different cries may sound like noise to someone else, but a mother hears them and understands.

If you listen to the noise of history, you must listen closely to hear the sounds of those who have turned the tide of history. History is filled with the babble of people who have gone before us and made big noises that amounted to very little.

Listen to the noise of today; it's the noise of disco and rock music, the noise of glasses clinking, and the noise of empty words on TV. If there has ever been an empty-hearted, empty-headed generation, it's the generation of today. We are an empty culture; a skeleton giving off noises of its own defeat.

This nation of ours, this generation of ours, has no guiding North Star. It has thrown out the Bible, and those who still have it are debating whether or not it's inerrant, all the time avoiding its authority. Some have listened to the sound of this day and followed the siren songs only to be swamped by despair. The harvest is plentiful, and it's a harvest of bitter seeds and fruit in our own lives. We have not found one way to eradicate sin, but we've listened to everything the world has had to say to us. We've listened to the wrong notes and we've danced to the wrong tune.

The trouble with too many people is that they can't distinguish the music of heaven from the music of the world. We can't dance to two tunes at the same time; we can't dance to the rhythm of the world with the left foot and move and march as a person of God with the right foot. We can't live in two camps; we can't serve two masters; we can't have our hearts tangled up with the world and our feet tangled up with God. It won't work.

123

What are you hearing? Are you listening for the voice of God through all the noise and clamor?

Prayer: *Be still, my soul, and listen for the voice of God. His voice is speaking; He has plans for me. O Lord, I pray for listening ears finely tuned to understand Your voice. Amen.*

VOICES OF OUR DAY

78. The Listening Ear

Psalm 115:2, 5a *Why do the nations say, "Where is their God?" . . . they have ears, but cannot hear . . .*
Matthew 11:15 *He who has ears, let him hear.*

In today's pampered society, not only do we have trouble distinguishing the message from the noise, but we also frequently listen to the wrong messengers. We listen too much to the mobs and the crowd; remember, they're the ones who cried, "Crucify him!"

Most of the voices of our day come from those who don't have enough blood on them. Their hands are clean and soft, with no nail prints; their feet are well shod, with socks up over the calves. The voices we hear are glib and polished. You don't learn anything from those who have been in power; you learn from those who have been in the trenches.

If you want to know about life and death, don't get a book on psychology; talk to a widow. If you want to know about loneliness, talk to a single woman who goes back to the same apartment she left in the morning, knowing that the coffee cup and paper are exactly where she left them. If you want to know something about fear, don't talk to some glib writer of mysteries; talk to the old. You don't know what fear is, until you wonder if your health is going to last as long as your social security. You don't know what fear is, until you wonder if you can afford to live at all. If you want to know about fear and desperation, talk to a parent whose adolescent is addicted to drugs and/or alcohol.

Help groups for different life situations have been founded, so that people in similar circumstances can give each other support. There are groups for single parents, for widows and widowers, for addicts and their families, and for cancer victims and their families. Only a person who has walked a similar road can understand the raw suffering, the throbbing pain in the inner being; only a fellow traveler can comprehend the torment of anger, grief, and shame that is a part of the human reaction to pain. One of God's most generous gifts to us is the gift of friends, those who can support and walk with us through a situation. Not only do we enjoy this gift for ourselves, but we can, in turn, be that support for someone else. This is God incarnate.

Prayer: *Father, my pain is great, and yet I know You are with me, because You have suffered pain and humiliation, desolation and temptation. I approach Your presence with confidence, to find grace and mercy to help me in my time of trouble. Amen.*

VOICES OF OUR DAY

79. The Mark of God

Matthew 27:46 *About the ninth hour Jesus cried out in a loud voice, "Eloi; Eloi, lama Sabachthani?" which means, "My God, my God, why have you forsaken me?"*
Hebrews 4:15,16 *For we do not have a high priest who is unable to sympathize with our weaknesses, but we have one who has been tempted in every way, just as we are – yet was without sin. Let us then approach the throne of grace with confidence, so that we may receive mercy and find grace to help us in our time of need.*

Several years ago, we received some papers of historical value, which had to do with land transactions. They dated back to the early settling of this country. You could look at them and trace the primitive style in which land had been transacted. One document in particular stood out. Down at the bottom of the deed was a mark where the signature should have been. It was made during a time when people who couldn't write made such marks to represent their names; but this particular mark was a cross, instead of the more common "X." Perhaps this person was so illiterate that he didn't even know how to make an "X," but he had at least made "his mark."

Follow us back even farther than this early American deed. Come back with us two thousand years. Come back to a hill on the suburb of Jerusalem. See not an "X" but a cross. That cross says, "God, His mark." In this world, we shall have tribulation; that's the cross.

Come with us three days hence and see an open tomb. It's not a very beautiful sight, just an open tomb. But the shadow of the cross falls upon it: "God, His mark."

Come with us a few days later and see an empowered church going out into the face of Rome. Again, this is "God, His mark." Come with us and see forgiven people, whose lives have been made clean. Look at the light in their eyes, the light of that Galilean who makes strength come alive. Look into the faces of people whose lives have been made right, and see "God, His mark."

Listen to the only voice that can cut through the ages in its authority — the voice that comes from nail-pierced hands and blood on the brow. The only life that is scarred enough and bloody enough to talk to us is the life of that Galilean, who promised to go with us through the valley of the shadow of death. Are you listening? Is the mark of God in your life?

Prayer: *Father, I thank You for the marks You leave for us. Thank You for carrying me when I cannot walk another step. Thank You for the mark of joy, the open tomb. Because of the open tomb I can face today, tomorrow, and whatever life may bring. Amen.*

THE SEARCH FOR WHOLENESS

80. The Search

Exodus 33:13 *Moses said to the Lord. . . . "If I have found favor in your eyes, teach me your ways, so I may know you and continue to find favor with you."*

In an old John Wayne movie called *The Searchers*, a group of cowboys searches for a young woman who was kidnapped by Indians. The movie makes you feel as though you're going to spend most of your life searching for something without ever knowing if you'll find it.

That's the way a lot of people go through life. They're always searching, but never quite sure if they're going to find the things they're looking for. You may be someone who is searching for a vocation, or a student searching through the library of experiences, or a young adult who feels driven to live out different lifestyles, trying them on as one tries on a dress or coat.

Moses, too, was searching, but he was searching for an intimate relationship with God. This search had driven him back up the mountain. Up to the time of the golden calf experience, there had been an intimacy between Moses and the people. But when they sinned so terribly, and had to be punished, Moses began spending more time in intimacy with God. This is when his desire to know God at a deeper level began to grow. The Bible gives a beautiful insight into the worship habits of Moses.

He pitched a tent some distance outside the camp and called it the "tent of meeting." Whenever Moses went out to the tent, all the people stood at the entrances to their tents and watched. As he went into the tent, the pillar of cloud would come down and stay at the entrance while the Lord spoke with Moses. "The Lord would speak to Moses face to face, as a man speaks with his friend." That is what we all want — friendship with God. We can have it if we pay the price — the price of time set aside for God, for regular worship habits, for Bible study. Moses didn't just stay in the tent all the time. After talking to God, he went out renewed to do his work. The people honored his time with God and benefited from his example of dedication.

Prayer: *Dear Father, how wonderful it would be to have it said of me, "The Lord spoke to (your name) face to face, as a man speaks with his friend." I want that intimate relationship. Give me the commitment to do my part. Amen.*

THE SEARCH FOR WHOLENESS

81. The Backside of God

Exodus 33:17,18 *And the Lord said to Moses, "I will do the very thing you have asked, because I am pleased with you and I know you by name." Then Moses said, "Now show me your glory."*

Moses was up the mountain again after the golden calf incident, when he broke the first tablets God gave. He was trying to receive again the law of God to take down to the people. He was wrestling with God emotionally and spiritually as he interceded for the people, for God was going to leave them right there. Moses implored God not to take His hand off the people. In the midst of this experience, as they talked to one another, God gave Moses the Ten Commandments again. He was ready to go back down the mountain after this time of intimacy with God, but before he went, he turned and said, "Now show me your glory."

The word "glory" in the Old Testament has a myriad of meanings. It means, "give me a new experience; give me a deep understanding of You; God, I want to know more about You." God says He will show as much of Himself as Moses can take, but He cannot give all of Himself. It would be like looking into the sun with nothing to filter it out, or like standing in front of a thousand searchlights, multiplied by infinity. It would be an impossible thing to receive, so God directed Moses to a cleft in a rock. God put His hands over the cleft of the rock where Moses was. Then God walked by and, as He did, He took away His hand. Moses saw the glory of God, but he did not see God full-faced; he saw the backside of God. But that was enough. The Bible says that Moses came down from the mountain and his face was aglow — it was so bright that he had to put some kind of veil over it to keep the glow from bothering the people.

We can never stand to see God face to face. Beware of anyone who knows all there is to know about God, because no one can probe the deepest parts of the mind of God. Man cannot absorb the fullness of God, and that is what the scripture is trying to tell us. It was a merciful act on the part of God when He let Moses see His back, for it was as much as Moses could take.

Have you ever seen a sunset that was so beautiful that you hardly could speak? Have you ever heard a symphony orchestra or a choir or an organ whose music brought tears to your eyes? Have you ever read a play or a novel that gave you understanding which you never had before? Have you ever had a teacher who pulled back the veil and gave you a view that you had never experienced? These are all part of the backside of God.

Sometimes we look over our shoulders and wonder why God lets things happen as they do. But the important thing is to see through the tangled web of chaotic experiences, and to know that God was there all the while, that the footprints of God are walking through our lives.

Prayer: *Father, I pray that You will help me learn to see Your footsteps in my life. Thank You for the signs of Your Glory, Now I need help through this situation (write down whatever is troubling you – your marriage, children, grandchildren, aging parents, loss of job, or whatever). Let God carry this for you. Amen.*

THE SEARCH FOR WHOLENESS

82. The Cleft of the Rock

Exodus 33:21,22 *Then the Lord said, "There is a place near me where you may stand on a rock. When my glory passes by, I will put you in a cleft in the rock and cover you with my hand until I have passed by."*

When we were growing up, two hymns frequently were sung by our congregation: "Rock of Ages, Cleft for Me," and "He Hideth My Soul in the Cleft of the Rock." Few people probably knew what a cleft was, but the words of those songs were indelibly etched on many minds.

Several years ago, during one of our visits to Israel, we drove through the Sinai desert and climbed Mount Sinai. It was the coldest day in fifty years in that part of the world, and it was raining hard.

After looking at the ruins and while waiting for the others, we went over to a big rock and sat down behind it. All of a sudden, it was as though we had walked into the calm of the storm. The temperature was warm, and we knew for the first time what it meant to be in the cleft of a rock.

Some of you may have been out in such a storm, and you have felt the wind and rain pelting in your face. You wonder how much business harassment, how much personal torment, how much family strife you can stand.

God never says that He will take you out of such turmoil, but the New Testament says that we will have God's presence in the midst of a storm; but do not be deluded. Jesus said that, in this world, we will have tribulation, but He has overcome the world. He hides us in our toughest times in the cleft of the rock, but we have to follow. Whatever footprints, whatever backside, whatever revelation of Him we can see, we follow Him through it.

God doesn't come and give you a road map, saying go this way or that. He comes and says, "Follow my back side, as I go ahead of you. I'll give you some protection when you need it, but I'll never show you the whole score card. I'll give you a glimpse of me as we go along, and you follow the glimpse."

We are still living with only the gimpse of the back side of God, but those who know Jesus Christ as Savior have had a chance to see a fuller revelation of God than we could ever have hoped for. Jesus Christ is God in the flesh. God came in the flesh to reveal Himself. If you want to know what God is like, look at Jesus. "He who has seen me, has seen the Father."

Prayer: *Thank You, Father, for the cleft in the rock that You so graciously provide for us. Open my eyes, my heart and mind that I may catch a glimpse of Your glory. Amen.*

THE SEARCH FOR WHOLENESS

83. Reflect the Glory

Exodus 34:29 *When Moses came down from Mount Sinai with the two tablets of the Testimony in his hands, he was not aware that his face was radiant because he had spoken with the Lord.*

Have you ever wondered why Michelangelo represented Moses with horns? The descriptions of Moses, "his face was radiant" or "the skin of his face shone," have a different meaning from what we assume. "Shine" in this case means, "to send out horns." It is translated here to mean, "to send out rays."

Moses was not aware of this radiance. Later he realized that it frightened the people, so he wore a veil when he was among them. He reflected the glory of God in his very being. We are given this narrative of Moses for a purpose. It proves to us that we do reflect that which we worship.

What do you see reflected in the faces of those around you? Too often, we see the reflection of greed and avarice, of hostility or fear, or of self-worship. Jesus understood how this worked when He gave his disciples the petitions of prayer to guide their communion with God. When He said to pray, "Hallowed be Thy name," He was saying to make God holy and to reflect His holiness in our lives.

Does your face shine? Are you a radiant testimony to the reflective glory of God in the life of a Christian? Look at yourself and decide what people are seeing in you.

Prayer: *Dear Father in heaven, I really do not like what I see in the mirror. I realize I am reflecting things that are not holy in my life. I want to pray with the words of the hymn, "Let others see Jesus in me." My life is a book and others are reading it. I don't want them to read unfit things. Amen.*

THE SEARCH FOR WHOLENESS

84. Guilt — No Hiding Place

Exodus 32:30 . . . Moses said to the people, "You have committed a great sin [the worship of the golden calf]. But now I will go up to the Lord; perhaps I can make atonement for your sin."
Exodus 32a Moses said, "But now, please forgive their sin . . ."
Exodus 32:34 "Now go, lead the people to the place I spoke of . . . However, when the time comes for me to punish, I will punish them for their sin."

The Scriptures are very clear about two things relating to guilt: One, you cannot hide it, and two, you cannot hide *from* it. No matter where you go, the hound of heaven is there. Hell is portable, and it is part of you. You may move from one place to another, but your guilt moves with you. You cannot escape the consequences of an indiscretion or an ill-advised action. You cannot get away from people you have hurt, or the bad things you have done. They hover over you all the time and dominate your life.

That message is often repeated in the Bible. God wanted Jonah to go one place, but Jonah decided to go across an ocean to get away from God. God grabbed him and brought him back, saying that he couldn't get away. Look at Jacob crossing the desert to get away from the brothers whom he had wronged. God appeared to him and told him he had to go back and face his brothers. Or look at Judas. He didn't cross an ocean or a desert, but he crossed the city to get away from Jesus, whom he betrayed. And Simon Peter crossed a courtyard trying to get away from Jesus, because he denied Him and the guilt was overwhelming.

Are you running? Are you hiding? There is nothing that you have done that is so bad that God cannot forgive. There is no place you can run to that is too far for God to see. There is no hiding place. Stop your running and your hiding, and let God heal you now.

Prayer: *Father, I am overwhelmed with guilt over these things: (write down whatever is troubling you). Help me to be able to accept forgiveness and to go on with a better life. Thank You for Moses who taught us so much. And thank You most of all for Jesus, Your son, who has made all things right. Amen.*